THE
FORGOTTEN HEROES
The Story of the Buffalo Soldiers

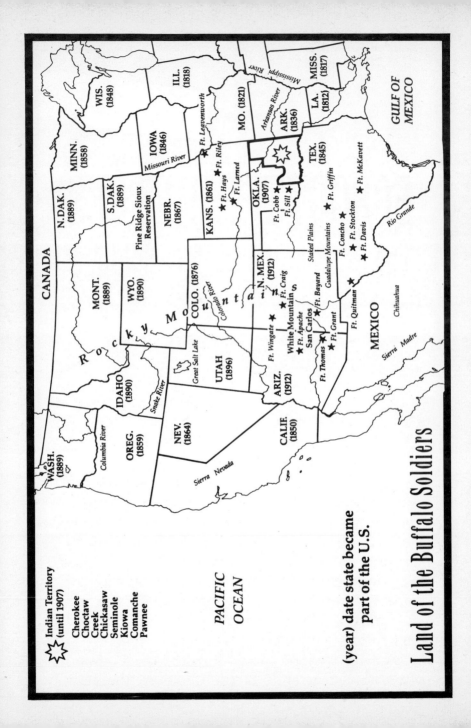

Land of the Buffalo Soldiers

THE
FORGOTTEN HEROES
The Story of the Buffalo Soldiers

CLINTON COX

A
LITTLE APPLE
PAPERBACK

SCHOLASTIC INC.
New York Toronto London Auckland Sydney

ISBN 0-590-45122-7

12 11 10 9 8 7   3   0 1/0

Printed in the U.S.A.   40

Contents

Introduction   vii

  1. The Moon of the Changing
     Seasons   1
  2. The Moon When the Deer Paw
     the Earth   19
  3. The Moon of Strong Cold   34
  4. The Moon of Popping Trees   46
  5. The Moon When the Ponies Shed   57
  6. The Hot Weather Begins Moon   72
  7. The Moon of the Red Blooming
     Lilies   85
  8. The Moon of Deer Horns Drop-
     ping Off   96
  9. The Hawk Moon   112
 10. The Time of the Buffalo Soldiers   137

Epilogue   159
Black Congressional Medal of Honor
  Winners in the West   165
Bibliography   169
Index   175

Introduction

Most of the great myths of the American West were born following the end of the Civil War in 1865.

From that time until the "Indian frontier" was officially declared closed in 1890, because it had become too settled, the popular imagination was captured by the deeds of cowboys, homesteaders, outlaws, cavalrymen, and great Native American chiefs and warriors such as Sitting Bull, Crazy Horse, Cochise, and Geronimo.

The history of that era and the legends that flowed from it continue to fascinate us, but some of the most important participants are strangely missing: the black men and women who were an integral part of the "Wild West."

They rode the range as cowboys and built homesteads on the prairie. They shot it out with the bad guys as United States marshals, and robbed and killed as outlaws.

A black explorer and fur trapper named Edward Rose served as chief of the Crows in the early

1800's and helped open the Missouri River for exploration toward the Rocky Mountains.

Another black "mountain man," James Beckwourth, found a pass in the Sierra Nevada Mountains that was unknown to whites, and Beckwourth Pass was soon used by hundreds of thousands of settlers as they traveled to California.

Beckwourth, like thousands of other black men and women, traveled across much of the West and was befriended by the people he met, including the Blackfeet and Crows. Like Rose, he was chosen by the Crows to be their chief and lived with them for several years.

But of all the black people who have disappeared from the history of the West, none played a larger role than the thousands of black cavalrymen who rode to the rescue of settlers, escorted wagon trains, carried the mail when no one else could get through, and fought warriors led by Geronimo, Satanta, Victorio, Mangas, Roman Nose, and other great leaders.

"Buffalo Soldiers," they were called by the warriors they fought. The first fort they were assigned to — Fort Leavenworth, Kansas — was named after a man Edward Rose had served under as a temporary officer decades before the black cavalrymen came west: Colonel Henry Leavenworth.

In many ways the story of the Buffalo Soldiers is the most fascinating of all the stories from that era, and certainly it is one of the most tragic.

Though a war had just been fought that ended slavery, black people found little acceptance and few opportunities in post-Civil War America. Many young black men joined the United States Army in their search for a freedom most had never known. But in becoming part of the army, they helped take freedom away from people who had always known it.

Their search took them west where Native Americans, who had been steadily losing land to whites for decades, were fighting to hold on to their final refuge: the Great Plains.

In that vast land, men of two outcast races met in battle on desert, plain, and mountain for over twenty years, while a government that hated them both imposed white domination over them and their people.

By the time their wars were over, many Native Americans had joined in helping to herd their brothers and sisters onto reservations. The final result was a country that was safe for white settlement but, at the same time, barely tolerated blacks or the Lakotas, Cheyennes, Apaches, and others who called this land their home.

While black soldiers were fighting Native Americans in the West, black men, women, and children were being lynched, segregated, and disenfranchised in the East. The government the soldiers fought for in the Great Plains rarely lifted a finger to help the soldiers' relatives at home and often joined in their oppression.

Men often make strange choices in their efforts to survive. In the United States of the late 1800's, both blacks and Native Americans were forced to make their choices in a country that offered them little to choose from.

Members of both groups fought to protect their homes and families, but by the time the Indian Wars were over, both blacks and Native Americans had lost.

Even in defeat, though, they suffered no disgrace. In the face of the government's determination to drive them to the fringes of society, they often acted with incredible heroism and an integrity that deserves our honor.

This is the story of the Buffalo Soldiers who fought during that legend-making time and of the men they fought. In the end, forces beyond the control of either group, including the wholesale slaughter of the buffalo and the unrelenting tide of white settlement, largely dictated the outcome of their struggle.

May this book be worthy of the men on both sides who lived the history of those desperate years when one way of life was destroyed and another planted on its ruins; when good men fought good men in one of history's greatest human dramas, and one of its most ironic.

The Moon of the Changing Seasons

Throughout the summer and fall of 1867, men of the 10th United States Cavalry Regiment rode out of forts in eastern Kansas, heading west toward lands that were home to the Cheyennes, Arapahos, Crows, Shoshones, and Lakotas (Sioux).

Far to the south at the same time, men of the 9th U.S. Cavalry Regiment rode into the vastness of western and southwestern Texas, home of the Comanches and their allies, the Kiowas.

The cavalrymen were mostly raw, young recruits from the East, strangers to the immense expanse of mountain, desert, and prairie they were now about to fight and die in: over one million square miles stretching from the cold, windswept mountains of Montana in the north, to the desolate and arid Staked Plains of Texas in the south; from the foothills of the Rocky Mountains in the west, to the grasslands stretching toward the Mississippi valley in the east.

The men in the 9th and 10th Cavalry were about to begin over three decades of continuous service in the West, a longer unbroken period of duty than that performed by any other regiment in the U.S. Army. During all that time they protected settlers; guarded telegraph, stagecoach, and railroad lines; carried the mail when no one else could get through; and chased cattle rustlers, Mexican bandits, and outlaws such as Billy the Kid.

Most of all, however, they fought Native American warriors led by Victorio, Naiche, Mangas, Geronimo, and other great men.

The soldiers in the 9th and 10th were the same as the rest of the cavalrymen who fought on the western frontier, except in one respect: they were the first black soldiers in the history of the United States Regular Army. They were the "Buffalo Soldiers," a term of respect that would soon be given them by the warriors they fought.

In 1866, Congress debated whether or not to allow black men to be part of the "Indian fighting'" army about to be sent to the West.

"At the present time settlements are springing up with unusual rapidity in the district of country between the Missouri river and the Pacific ocean, where heretofore the Indian was left in undisputed possession," said Lieutenant General Ulysses S. Grant, commander of the army.

"Emigrants are pushing to those settlements and to the gold fields of the Rocky mountains, by every available highway. The people flocking to those regions are citizens of the United States, and are entitled to the protection of the government. They are developing the resources of the country to its great advantage, thus making it the interest as well as duty to give them military protection. This makes a much greater force west of the Mississippi necessary than was ever heretofore required."

Though more than 180,000 black men had served in the Union Army during the Civil War, and more than 38,000 had died, they were barred from enlisting in the regular army and placed instead in volunteer regiments. Now that the Civil War was over, many congressmen wanted to continue to keep the regular army all-white.

One congressman, fearing that black soldiers would be stationed in the East, argued that "they could perform no military duty that could not better be performed by white men; that they were not wanted at the north, and that at the south they would prove a continual source of irritation, complaint and disquiet."

A congressman from Delaware said that "their presence in a community would be a stench in the nostrils of the people."

Several congressmen favored enlisting black men, however, because of a combination of moral and practical reasons.

The *Congressional Globe* summarized their arguments as follows: "If it was a privilege to serve in the army these troops had earned it by their gallantry [in the Civil War], and if it was a duty they should not be allowed to shirk it. They were as good as other troops, and were less liable to desert, their opportunities for advancement in civil pursuits being less than among the whites."

General Grant said that although he was not recommending "the permanent employment of colored troops," he had no objection to their use and thought they could probably "be obtained more readily than white ones."

Grant noted that all the white volunteers who had been forced to stay in the army after the end of the Civil War "have become dissatisfied . . . and, by reason of dissatisfaction, they are no longer of use and might as well be discharged at once — every one now remaining in service. The colored volunteer has equal right to claim his discharge, but as yet he has not done so."

And so, partly because of a desire to see justice done and partly because they knew black men would be less likely to desert because they had few opportunities in civilian life, Congress voted to enlist six (later reduced to four) black regiments to fight in the "Wild West."

The act, passed on July 28, 1866, resulted in the formation of the 9th and 10th Cavalry and the 24th and 25th Infantry. All the regiments had white officers.

With passage of the 1866 law, many young black men flocked to enlist for five-year terms at $13 a month. They were men who had met with widespread discrimination in the North and with wholesale white violence in the South, as they tried to build new lives in the aftermath of the Civil War.

White southerners were determined to continue treating black people as slaves, even though the Civil War had ended slavery.

Near Pine Bluff, Arkansas, a black settlement was attacked. The next morning, a man who came on the scene said he found "a sight that apald me 24 Negro men woman and children were hanging to trees all round the Cabbins."

The incident was not unusual.

An ex-slave named Henry Adams said "over 2,000 colored people" were murdered in the area around Shreveport, Louisiana, in 1865 alone.

The law establishing the "peacetime" army called for the black regiments to be composed, as far as possible, of men "who had served two years during the war [Civil War] and had been distinguished for capacity and good conduct in the field."

The first men to join the 9th and 10th included veterans like Jacob Wilks, whose parents escaped from slavery while he was still a baby. Wilks fought in the Union Army and was present when Confederate General Robert E. Lee surrendered to General Ulysses S. Grant at Appomattox Courthouse in Virginia.

George Washington Williams of Pennsylvania

(soon to be made the 10th's first sergeant major) was also a veteran of the Union Army, participating in several battles before being wounded in Virginia in 1864. He also fought as an artillery lieutenant in the Mexican Revolutionary Army that toppled Emperor Maximilian in 1867.

Williams said he then went home, found himself longing "for the outdoor, lively, exhilarating exercise of military life," and joined the 10th.

There were also many recruits who had no military experience, such as nineteen-year-old Emanuel Stance of East Carroll Parish, Louisiana, who enlisted although he was barely five feet tall. Stance left his home in the Mississippi Delta on a sunny day in October 1866 and spent the next twenty years as a cavalryman in the West.

Another recruit was George Jordan, who was a nineteen-year-old farmer from Kentucky when he enlisted on Christmas Day, 1866. Jordan would stay in the army for thirty years, fighting in Texas, New Mexico, Arizona, Indian Territory (most of present-day Oklahoma), and finally, on the Pine Ridge Sioux Reservation in South Dakota.

Reuben Waller was a twenty-seven-year-old ex-slave who had been forced to accompany his owner, a Confederate general, through twenty-nine battles in the Civil War. Waller was present at Fort Pillow, Tennessee, when Confederate soldiers massacred captured black soldiers from the Union Army.

Waller developed "a great liking" for the Union cavalrymen he saw during the Civil War, and so, he said, "on the sixteenth day of July, 1867, I enlisted for the Indian war that was then raging in Kansas and Colorado."

One man, reflecting the sentiments of many other black youths who joined the cavalry, said: "I got tired of looking mules in the face from sunrise to sunset. Thought there must be a better livin' in this world."

George Goldsby of Selma, Alabama, and George W. Ford, who grew up on a farm next to George Washington's Mount Vernon, Virginia, estate, were two more of the almost 2,000 men who joined the 9th and 10th in 1866 and 1867.

The men came from several states and many walks of life.

A typical group of 100 recruits in the 9th showed the following occupations: 51 soldiers (apparently men who had served in the Union Army), 23 laborers, 14 farmers, 2 teamsters, and a painter, cook, sailor, hostler, and miller.

The largest group of men came from Louisiana (36) and Kentucky (17), but there were also men from Virginia, Mississippi, Alabama, Tennessee, North Carolina, Georgia, Florida, Pennsylvania, Maryland, and Arkansas.

Their ages ranged from 18 to 34, with 20- and 21-year-olds accounting for almost half the men. Many of them had once been slaves.

A similar group of 100 recruits in the 10th showed a much wider diversity, both geographically and in their occupations.

Laborers (39) and farmers (29) were the two largest groups, followed by soldiers and waiters (6 each); sailors (4), boatmen, engineers, and cooks (3 each); barbers, hostlers, and servants (2 each); and one mason.

The largest numbers came from Virginia (13), Kentucky (12), and Missouri (10), but there were also residents of New York, Massachusetts, Connecticut, Pennsylvania, Alabama, Maryland, Ohio, New Jersey, North Carolina, South Carolina, Louisiana, Tennessee, Arkansas, Texas, Georgia, and the District of Columbia.

There was even one man who was born in the Cherokee Nation in Indian Territory; another from Halifax, Nova Scotia; and a third who was born in Leavenworth, Kansas — almost within sight of the fort that would be the 10th's first home.

The ages of the men in the 10th ranged from eighteen to thirty-five, but most were in their early twenties.

The majority had never known slavery, but they knew the sting of the racial prejudice that kept them from being accepted as full American citizens.

It was especially ironic, then, that these men joined regiments specifically created to fight Native Americans: people fighting for the same things

the black men had fought for all their lives —
homes of their own and the opportunity to live
their lives in peace.

Many of the new recruits, in fact, had been
taught from childhood about the injustices done
to Native Americans.

"We remembered of having read in some
Sunday-school book that it is wrong to persecute
the poor Indian," said George Williams, talking
of the soldiers' conversation their first night on
the prairie, "that he owned the whole country;
that the white people would have to answer for
their wickedness in the Day of Judgment."

But the chance of a steady paycheck and, for
some, the excitement and adventure they hoped
to find in the "Wild West" outweighed any qualms
they may have felt about fighting other struggling,
dark-skinned people.

There was little any warrior had to fear from
these young black cavalrymen at first, however,
for many of them were so raw they couldn't stay
in their saddles.

"What followed beggars all description," wrote
Williams of the first attempt by his Company L
men to mount their horses.

"We didn't know what to say or do. We heard
sabers and canteens rattle; heard horses squeal and
men 'cuss,' and saw new boots and recruits flying
in the air; everywhere we looked we saw horses
flying, some had unceremoniously deposited their

riders, or would-be riders, on *terra firma* . . .

"Some had riders on them who were religiously and pathetically pleading with their ungovernable steed to be careful of the trees and of other obstructions! When we came to ourselves we ordered all the men we could find to 'git off of their critters' as best they could.

"Some of the men came back riding, some walking; some had caps, some had no caps. . . . Some of the horses came back, some never came back . . ."

The men were trained hard, however, and were soon "being clothed, armed, drilled, mounted and sent out on the Plains as fast as they arrived" in Kansas, Williams reported.

The army high command desperately wanted more troops in the field, as white encroachment on Native American lands led to more and more violence. That violence still seemed far away to the young cavalrymen, however.

The first night out from Fort Riley, Williams and the rest of his company "relished our supper," then "laid down to dream of the red man and the bison." They also remembered what they had learned in Sunday school.

"We felt that if there was an Indian near we would run and fall upon his neck and weep," Williams recalled.

But the reality was that they were in an army that was not about to weep over "an Indian," no matter what the Sunday school book said.

The lands they were about to fight and die in had once belonged solely to Native Americans. Now white settlers were staking out homes and farms, contractors were building roads, and the army was erecting forts, driving the Lakotas, Cheyennes, and other original inhabitants into smaller and smaller areas.

Led by a huge warrior named Roman Nose, who fasted and prayed before going into battle, many Cheyennes and Arapahos vowed to fight to hold onto their land in the plains of Colorado and Kansas.

Kiowas and Comanches under Satanta and other leaders fought desperately to retain their hunting grounds, which stretched from southern Kansas into Colorado, New Mexico, and Indian territories.

In the north, in what is now Montana and Wyoming, a forty-five-year-old Lakota war chief named Red Cloud led his warriors against a string of army forts built to protect settlers and miners.

One of the warriors who followed Red Cloud was a young man who sought guidance before battle by going on solitary vigils in the hills. His people called him Our Strange Man but he called himself Tashunka Witko, Crazy Horse.

Sometimes Crazy Horse was joined in battle by a thirty-five-year-old man who had been called Hunk-es-ni, or Slow, as a child. Now he was an increasingly respected warrior, religious leader, and hunter named Tatanka Yotanka, the Sitting Bull.

In April 1867, as the first of the black cavalrymen rode onto the Great Plains, General Winfield Scott Hancock launched a campaign to "overawe" the warriors. Instead, he provoked a full-scale war.

Hancock had his 1,400 troops, led by Lieutenant Colonel George Armstrong Custer, burn over 250 lodges and everything else Roman Nose and his people owned. Custer then pursued the fleeing men, women, and children, but they managed to escape.

The plains exploded in war from one end to the other, and the raw, young recruits rode right into the explosion.

On August 1, 1867, a railroad worker raced into Fort Hays, Kansas, a post that had been established less than two months before to protect construction crews building the Kansas Pacific Railroad.

"A hundred Cheyennes attacked our camp and scalped seven men!" he cried.

Thirty-four of the black troopers quickly saddled up and raced thirteen miles to the camp. The raiders were gone, but the soldiers followed their trail till dark, then returned to camp.

The next morning, as they moved cautiously near the Saline River, scores of screaming warriors suddenly burst from the thick growth in front of them.

The men formed groups of four as they had been taught to do when attacked. One man held the horses' reins and passed out ammunition, while the other three fired at the charging warriors.

There was hand-to-hand fighting, with tomahawks and sabers slashing the air under a burning sun. Many of the troopers were wounded, and their ammunition was running low.

"After a severe engagement of two hours," wrote one man, "the command discovered a large herd of buffalo, as they thought, coming over a hill, which proved another large band of Indians, who promptly joined in the attack, when a retreat was ordered."

The men mounted their horses, with some riding double because so many of the horses had been killed. The soldiers broke through the circle of warriors and headed for the railroad camp, pursued by a force of almost 300 Cheyennes.

"After six hours of hard fighting," the soldier reported, "the troop [company] was able to strike bottom land, fifteen miles distant, where relief was obtained."

The conduct of the men, he said, "is spoken of in the highest terms."

The 10th lost its first man in action that day: Sergeant William Christy. The twenty-one-year-old farmer from Mercersburg, Pennsylvania, had been in the army less than two months.

Three weeks later, the black soldiers crossed paths for the first time with Satanta and the Kiowas and Comanches he led.

Satanta was a barrel-chested man who painted his face and body with brilliant red paint and tied red streamers on his medicine lance before going into battle.

About forty of the soldiers were out scouting the area around Fort Hays, Kansas, with ninety members of the 18th Kansas Volunteer Cavalry, searching for a wagon train that was reportedly under attack.

The men had just entered a ravine when gunshots and arrows came whistling at them. Within minutes, fourteen men were killed or wounded, and twenty-five horses lay dead.

The main body of troops heard the shooting and hurried toward the sounds, said one soldier, "when suddenly a large force of several hundred Indians swooped down upon it from every direction."

Red streamers flying, Satanta charged into battle blowing a French horn and wearing a U.S. Army major-general's uniform given him by Hancock a few weeks before.

"The command was immediately rallied," declared the soldier, "wheeled by fours and . . . dismounted. Men were placed behind the banks and, surrounding the horses, opened fire, the fire of the enemy passing over the backs of the animals."

Satanta kept trying to break through the cavalrymen's defenses and drive off their horses, but was driven back each time. Satanta and his men stopped fighting when darkness came, but the men in the ravine were still trapped.

Temporarily unable to help their comrades, the other soldiers hurried off to search for the beseiged wagon train. They found it at dawn, but it was surrounded by several hundred warriors.

The soldiers broke through their lines, rescued the train, and then rode back to try and save their friends in the ravine.

This time they succeeded "and soon returned with fifteen wounded men perched on five horses, which was all that was left out of thirty."

Satanta renewed the attack, and the fighting went on all day, with the soldiers again withdrawing when nightfall came.

Thirteen of the cavalrymen were wounded, and Private Thomas Smith, a house painter from Charleston, South Carolina, was killed and scalped.

The troopers had exhibited "remarkable coolness and bravery" during the fighting, their officers reported.

But though the men grieved over the newly made friends they had lost, they also took pride in a name the Cheyenne warriors had given them after the fight. Army scouts had crept up close to the main Cheyenne camp after the battle. They reported that the warriors spoke with grudging admiration about these new, dark-skinned cavalrymen they had fought for the first time. "Buffalo Soldiers," they called them.

The men involved in those first clashes were all from Company F. When they asked why the Cheyennes had given them that name, the scouts said the buffalo fought ferociously when cornered, as the soldiers had done.

The warriors must also have drawn comparisons between the hair of some of the soldiers and the hair of the buffalo. At any rate, the buffalo was sacred to the Native Americans of the Great Plains, and it is highly unlikely they would have given its name to soldiers they didn't respect.

The troopers in Company F proudly accepted their new name. Soon afterwards, other companies of the regiment were also called "Buffalo Soldiers" by the warriors they fought.

The term would eventually be used to refer to men in the 9th Cavalry as well, but for now it applied solely to the men of the 10th. When they designed their regimental flag, they placed a buffalo at the top of it.

All members of the regiment were now in the field.

The roster of the 10th listed 1,004 enlisted men and 32 officers by the end of October. The complexions of the men, said one of their officers, were black, brown, "and many as white as the whitest in the white regiments."

They were commanded by an ex-music teacher and Civil War hero named Colonel Benjamin Grierson. Grierson fought all attempts to treat his men as second-class soldiers and to give them inferior horses and equipment.

In early spring, when the general commanding Fort Leavenworth told him to take his "damned Mokes [a nineteenth-century derogatory term for black people] and camp outside the post," Grierson requested and received permission to move the regimental headquarters to Fort Riley.

"Colored troops will hold their place in the army of the United States as long as the government lasts," Grierson predicted.

The men of the 9th and 10th would remain in small, scattered units for most of the next thirty years, only rarely and briefly coming together in one place as they patrolled the enormous spaces assigned to them.

That summer, for instance, there were only three regular army cavalry regiments — the 3rd, Custer's 7th, and the 10th — patrolling the almost 300,000 square miles of Kansas, Missouri, Indian Territory, and New Mexico Territory (an area the army designated the Department of the Missouri).

The saga of the Buffalo Soldiers had begun.

From now until the frontier was officially considered closed in 1890, at least one in every five army cavalrymen who rode to the rescue of settlers, upheld the law when there was no one else to do so, and battled the elements in plains and mountains while following the trail of warriors, was black.

Sometimes, as in the summer of 1867 in the Department of the Missouri, one in every three was black.

They quickly made their presence felt.

That first summer, wrote a correspondent for *Harper's Weekly*, "the only effective fighting which has been done by our forces has been accomplished by the negro troops. . . .

"A few months since you could not have convinced a ranchman that there was 'any fight in the colored troops.' It is different now. I have not met a single frontiersman who has seen the dusky patriots 'go for Indians,' but is loud in their praise."

The Buffalo Soldiers were about to ride into history, and other dark-skinned men who would also ride into history awaited their coming on lands they and their fathers had lived on for generations, lands they had vowed to protect.

It was a fitting time for the legend of the Buffalo Soldiers to begin, for many lives were about to change.

It was October, the time Native Americans called the Moon of the Changing Seasons.

The Moon When the Deer Paw the Earth — 2

Thousands of warriors raced from behind a hill, lances and war shields held aloft, headdresses flying in the wind. There were Kiowas, Comanches, Southern Cheyennes, Arapahos, and Apaches. Women and children ran alongside the seemingly endless columns, laughing, shouting, and cheering.

The warriors raced toward army officers and civilans wearing stiff black suits, all seated in a beautiful grove of cottonwood trees beside a creek called Medicine Lodge.

The grove was in southern Kansas, just a few miles above the border with Indian Territory. Native Americans had long considered it a sacred place, a neutral meeting ground where healing could take place and no one would be attacked.

Now, at the request of the United States Government, the warriors had come to talk of peace.

General Hancock's disastrous campaign, combined with widespread anger at reports of the indiscriminate killing of Native Americans, led

Congress to create an Indian Peace Commission "to establish peace with certain hostile Indian tribes."

General William Tecumseh Sherman, commander of the Department of the Missouri, reluctantly consented to the commission when it became apparent he couldn't stop it. But he made no bones about what he wanted it to accomplish.

Sherman told the secretary of war the government should get the "hostile Indians" out of Kansas and southern Nebraska "as soon as possible, and it makes little difference whether they be coaxed out by Indian commissioners or killed."

So the commissioners had come to coax. With them were almost six hundred other whites, including newspaper reporters from around the country, congressmen, business leaders and Kit Carson, the famous scout who had helped drive the Navajos from their lands three years before. There were also many Buffalo Soldiers.

All of these men watched as the warriors wheeled to a halt in front of the officers and commissioners, pranced their horses before the silently watching men, then charged away while other warriors raced up to take their places.

Finally all the chiefs dismounted and sat in a circle under a huge tent with the officers and commissioners. A fire burned in the center, and one by one the chiefs rose to speak.

There was the flamboyant Satanta and Lone

Wolf of the Kiowas, Little Raven of the Arapahos, Ten Bears of the Comanches, Wolf Sleeve of the Kiowa-Apaches, and Black Kettle of the Southern Cheyennes.

Black Kettle had seen 105 of his women and children massacred by soldiers three years earlier at Sand Creek, Colorado, so he camped on the opposite side of Medicine Lodge Creek in case there was trouble.

After several days, a wary Roman Nose came riding in, leading several hundred warriors who fired their pistols and rifles into the air as they came.

The commissioners wanted the chiefs to sign a treaty removing their people to reservations in southern Kansas and Indian Territory.

Below the Arkansas River in southern Kansas, the Southern Cheyennes and Arapahos would be allowed to hunt buffalo and would be left alone "as long as grass grows and waters run." North of the river, whites could take the land, carve out their farms and towns, and build the railroad.

Satanta rose to speak. First he shook hands with each of the commissioners; then he said:

"I have heard that you intend to settle us on a reservation near the mountains. I don't want to settle. I love to roam over the prairies. There I feel free and happy. . . ."

The reporters who heard Satanta speak called him the "Orator of the Plains."

Ten Bears, who was described by listeners as more a poet than a warrior, said that when he visited Washington, D.C., President Ulysses S. Grant told him that "all the Comanche land was ours, and that no one should hinder us in living upon it. So why do you ask us to leave the rivers, and the sun, and the wind, and live in houses? . . . Do not speak of it more."

But most of the chiefs seemed to fear that Sherman spoke the truth when he told them the roads, railroad tracks, and white settlers would come into their lands no matter what they did.

"You can no more stop this," Sherman said, "than you can stop the sun or moon."

The chiefs debated with each other far into the night about the best course to follow for the good of their people. They resumed their discussions again the next day and for several days after that.

At last the majority of them signed, but Lone Wolf and Roman Nose refused.

The Cheyennes and Arapahos agreed to move south to share a reservation near Fort Larned, Kansas, while the Comanches and Kiowas agreed to leave Texas and share a reservation between the Red and Washita rivers in what is now western Oklahoma.

The Arkansas River would serve as a "deadline." South of the river the warriors could live as they had always lived and hunt the buffalo "so long as the buffalo may range thereon in such numbers as to justify the chase," while north of the river whites were free to settle.

Roman Nose and the warriors who followed him rode off, vowing to continue their fight for freedom. But for the time being, with winter coming on, there was peace on the plains.

Six companies of the 10th were assigned to Fort Riley for the winter, while several detachments from other companies continued to guard the railroad.

Company M, the Calico Troop, was moved to Fort Gibson, Indian Territory, near the northern part of the Cheyenne-Arapaho reservation. Sergeant Major Williams's company was put to work enlarging Fort Arbuckle in Indian Territory near the southern part of the reservation.

Williams had hoped to pass his time at a comfortable desk job at Fort Riley, "far away from the Indian's deadly arrow." But a newly arrived officer who was "thirsting for Indian blood" wanted to be assigned to the field, and the reluctant Williams was forced to go with him.

However, Williams and his comrades were destined to fight few warriors that first winter. Their enemies turned out to be boredom, whiskey bootleggers, cattle rustlers, outlaws, and the racial prejudice that remained with them throughout their careers.

One of the 10th's officers complained that the cavalrymen were forced to do more than their share of the heavy labor involved in rebuilding the fort. The officer was also angry because the post surgeon frequently used the black soldiers as orderlies and cooks when they went to the hospital as patients.

More important to their combat efficiency, however, was the condition of their horses.

When Colonel Grierson inspected the first fifty horses assigned to the regiment, he found that not one was fit for service. They were all either crippled or at least a dozen years old.

In the years to come, the unit was routinely given horses white cavalry regiments had already ruined or rejected. Custer's 7th Cavalry was usually given the pick of new horses; then the other white regiments were allowed to make their choices. The Buffalo Soldiers were forced to take whatever mounts were left over, and often there were not enough horses for all of them.

The soldiers' only recreation at Arbuckle was a primitive billiard hall built onto the post trader's store. On winter nights, when darkness came early and the wind howled across the plains, the men had little to do but huddle close to the stoves in their barracks.

Though the Buffalo Soldiers' rates of desertion were consistently much lower than those of white soldiers, the winter of 1867–68 saw many of the green recruits take their chances in desperate flight across the inhospitable land. Some died on the prairies, but, like many white soldiers, they were willing to risk death to escape the harsh land surrounding them. A few months earlier, thirty-five men deserted from Custer's regiment in a single day, with another ten fleeing the next day.

As Christmas neared, Grierson made plans for his men at Fort Riley to celebrate the holidays in the post recreation hall. Custer and his officers refused to share the hall with the black cavalrymen, however, so Grierson found an empty warehouse and scrounged lumber so the men could build benches and a stage.

(Custer disliked black people so much he refused to accept a commission in the 10th and lobbied successfully for appointment to a white regiment. He frequently defended slavery and, two years before, campaigned with President Andrew Johnson in the latter's attempt to stop Congress from giving black men the right to vote.)

Mrs. Grierson and other officers' wives talked the quartermaster into giving them several discarded blankets, which they then sewed into a large curtain for the stage. The regimental band practiced Christmas carols until Grierson and the band leader, a lieutenant who was also an ex-music teacher, were satisfied.

On Christmas Day, the men entered the warehouse and saw that it was decorated with ornaments, evergreens, and a huge Christmas tree. They held religious services, then sat down to a dinner of turkey, venison, tinned tomatoes and oysters, and plum pudding.

But the evening and the holidays ended all too quickly for the men, and the peace that had seemed so near at Medicine Lodge Creek began to recede.

Soon so many mail carriers were being murdered on their runs between Forts Arbuckle and Gibson that white men refused to take the job. Native American scouts were hired, and they carried the mail in teams of at least two. The Buffalo Soldiers were also pressed into this hazardous duty, as they would often be throughout the Great Plains in times of danger.

Private George W. Ford was one of the men chosen for this task, and quickly found himself spending "many hard winter days" riding the wind-swept plains of Indian Territory. Their assignment, according to orders from headquarters, was to keep "open commuications between Fts. Gibson and Arbuckle."

The twenty-year-old Ford said the couriers faced almost constant peril because, "besides fording the icy waters of the Canadian, the Washita, and Wild Horse, there was also the danger of capture by Indians."

Private Filmore Roberts, a twenty-one-year-old laborer who joined the regiment in Keokuk, Iowa, was another of those chosen for this arduous duty. He left Arbuckle for Gibson in midwinter, but never arrived. The officers listed him as a deserter.

On a warm day in spring, however, his comrades found his body floating in some willow trees in shallow water in the Canadian River. The mail pouch he had been entrusted with was still strapped to his back. The young private had died trying to complete his mission.

Other members of the regiment spent the winter of 1867–68 trying to track down white hunters who boldly and recklessly violated the treaty signed at Medicine Lodge. The hunters killed buffalo by the thousands, sold the hides, and left the bodies to rot on the prairie.

To make matters even worse for the Kiowas, Comanches, Cheyennes, and Arapahos who had moved to the reservations, Congress refused to honor the peace commission's promise to provide food, blankets, and other essentials called for in the treaty. Men, women, and children grew increasingly hungry, especially after the migrating buffalo drifted beyond the boundaries of the reservations.

Soon, increasing numbers of warriors were leaving the reservations to attack whites throughout Indian Territory and in northern and western Texas. They also attacked members of the five Civilized Tribes, so-called because they had taken up farming and adopted many aspects of white culture.

Whites had driven the Five Nations — the

Cherokees, Choctaws, Creeks, Chickasaws, and
Seminoles — off their lands in the Southeast in
the 1830's and 1840's and forcibly relocated them
to Indian Territory.

Thousands died as they traveled by foot, cart,
and horseback along what the Cherokees called
the "Trail Where They Cried," or the "Trail of
Tears," to the plains that were already inhabited
by the fiercely proud and still-free Kiowas and Comanches. Nonetheless, the newcomers were allowed to settle, and they were left alone, except
for occasional raids on their horses and cattle.

Now, with hunger stalking the reservations, anger came quickly to men who had only reluctantly
agreed to the peace terms at Medicine Lodge. They
watched their wives and children grow thinner,
and they felt betrayed. And so they lashed out at
those around them who possessed the land they
had once lived on and who possessed food while
the warriors and those they loved went hungry.

Private James Young, a farmer from Lafayette
County, Missouri, and almost one hundred other
Buffalo Soldiers were assigned to the Seminole
Agency to help protect the Five Nations from the
warriors' raids. Many members of the Five Nations,
especially the Seminoles, had intermarried with
black men and women.

The assignment was one the cavalrymen greeted
with mixed emotions, though. Some members of
the Civilized Tribes had owned slaves and fought

for the Confederacy during the Civil War, but others had sheltered escaping slaves in their villages and helped them escape to Canada.

The soldiers had little time to dwell on the past, however, because Kiowa and Comanche raids on the cattle herds of the Choctaws and Chickasaws were threatening to lead to open warfare.

The Buffalo Soldiers spent the winter at the agency trying to stop the violence. One time they left on a march of eighty miles to assist an agent "in reclaiming white children who were held captive by Indians."

While the Buffalo Soldiers were concentrating their efforts at the agency, Kiowa and Comanche hunters rode west into the Texas Panhandle in search of buffalo. More often than not they returned empty-handed. Entire herds had been slaughtered by white hunters equipped with long-range rifles with telescopes mounted on the barrels. Often the whites killed just for the fun of it.

The Kiowa and Comanche hunters found more and more of their old hunting grounds fenced off each time they went out. They also found ranches where there had been none before and heard rumors that another railroad (the Atchison, Topeka, and the Santa Fe) would soon run through the area.

Winter finally ended, and still the government had not delivered the promised food to those who signed the treaty. Hundreds of angry warriors

slipped away from the reservations. The Cheyennes and Arapahos struck at settlers in Colorado
and Kansas, while the Kiowas and Comanches
rode south to strike in Texas.

Several chiefs, including Black Kettle and Kicking Bird, still struggled for peace and urged their
people to remain on the reservations. But others
chose to lead their warriors on raids.

General Sherman warned them they could not
leave the reservations even if they and their families were starving.

"We have selected and provided reservations for
all, off the great road [the Santa Fe Trail]," Sherman declared. "All who cling to their old hunting
grounds are hostile and will remain so till killed
off."

Edward W. Wynkoop, the agent appointed to
oversee the distribution of food and supplies to the
Cheyennes, urged Black Kettle to be patient even
though the government had broken its promises
to his people.

"Our white brothers are pulling away from us
the hand they gave at Medicine Lodge," Black
Kettle replied, "but we will try to hold on to it.
We hope the Great Father will take pity on us and
let us have the guns and ammunition he promised
us so we can hunt buffalo to keep our families from
going hungry."

Wynkoop arranged for Black Kettle and other

chiefs to meet with General Philip Sheridan, who had replaced Hancock as commander of the Department of the Missouri. When Wynkoop asked if he could give arms to Black Kettle's warriors, Sheridan said angrily: "Yes, give them arms, and if they go to war my soldiers will kill them like men."

Stone Calf, one of the Cheyenne chiefs, replied: "Let your soldiers grow long hair, so that we can have some honor in killing *them*."

The summer of 1868 was more than half over before the government delivered the first of the food promised in the treaty. It consisted of salt pork, moldy cornmeal, and flour that was full of mouse droppings.

The anger of the warriors rose even higher.

More and more of them left the reservations to seek food and, in some cases, to seek revenge.

"I have just returned from northwestern Kansas, the scene of a terrible Indian massacre," Governor Samuel Crawford telegraphed President Johnson on August 17. "On the thirteenth and fourteenth, forty of our citizens were killed and wounded by hostile Indians."

Buffalo Soldiers were sent to scout for warriors along the Saline and Solomon rivers. Then, immediately on returning to camp, some were sent out again "under orders for duty on the Denver Stage route." This was a wagon road that led across

Kansas to the mining camps in neighboring Colorado Territory, and it was under almost constant siege.

Private Reuben Waller and sixty other Buffalo Soldiers rode to the rescue of settlers on the Saline River and hurriedly helped them build a protective blockhouse, as well as a corral for their horses and cattle.

Then the men were back in the saddle, riding hard to the scene of yet another reported attack. Before the month was over, Waller and his companions had ridden a total of 267 miles. They were outdone by the men in Company I, however, who covered 500 miles. All told, the Buffalo Soldiers of the 10th, sent out to protect settlers, rode an incredible 2,095 miles in less than a month as the summer of 1868 drew to a close.

Hundreds of miles to the south, the men of the 9th were also riding long and hard, on the trail of Comanches, Kiowas, Kickapoos, and Mescalero Apaches. Like the patrols of the 10th, those of the 9th often arrived after the swiftly moving warriors had already disappeared.

Sergeant George Jordan and the men under him, along with several other companies, chased war parties throughout western Texas. But their efforts were usually in vain. Several times, the warriors escaped by crossing the Rio Grande into Mexico, where the U.S. Army was not allowed to follow. By the end of the summer, eight Texas counties had been devastated by raids.

Politicians demanded that the army stop the attacks, and General Sheridan began to lay plans for a winter campaign to destroy Black Kettle and the Southern Cheyennes.

The chief and his people settled into their traditional wintering place between the Washita and the Canadian rivers, in southern Indian Territory.

Black Kettle still held out for peace, though he was increasingly unable to control his angry young warriors. To the north, Roman Nose — the chief who had spurned Black Kettle's pleas to give the whites what they wanted at Medicine Lodge — still roamed free.

Roman Nose and the warriors who followed him established a camp near the village of a Lakota chief named Pawnee Killer. One day several hunters came riding in and said that about fifty white men armed with long rifles were heading their way. The white men were dressed in rough leather clothing, and only three or four of them wore army uniforms.

Roman Nose was asked to lead the Cheyenne and Lakota warriors in an attack on these whites, and he agreed. To the south, Reuben Waller and his comrades were still patrolling the embattled Denver Post Road. Soon the paths of Roman Nose and the Buffalo Soliders would cross.

It was September, the Moon When the Deer Paw the Earth.

The Moon of Strong Cold

3

On September 15, 1868, one hundred Cheyennes attacked a unit of Buffalo Soldiers at Big Sandy Creek, Colorado, on the Denver Post Road.

The Cheyennes were members of the Hotami-tanio (Dog Soldier Society), the most feared and respected military society on the southern plains.

The fighting lasted all day and was often hand-to-hand, with dust swirling so thick it was hard to tell Buffalo Soldiers from Dog Soldiers.

Nightfall neared and at last the Cheyennes withdrew. They had lost eleven men. Seven soldiers were wounded, and ten of their horses were dead or captured. The cavalrymen, almost out of ammunition and many riding two to a horse, struggled under cover of darkness to Fort Wallace, Kansas, just a few miles east of the Colorado border.

Even after they reached the fort, daylight revealed "large parties of Indians in sight." The troopers were not attacked again, however. A few days later, written orders were issued commending them for their gallantry.

There were no replacement horses available for them, so another detachment of Buffalo Soldiers was sent to patrol the road. The seventy men, who were from Company H, were scheduled to be in the field a month and were accompanied by three officers and a doctor. There were also several frontiersmen for added strength in fighting the escalating attacks on travelers and wagon trains.

On the morning of September 23, according to Captain Louis Carpenter, the company commander, "We had reached a point on the old stage road about 45 miles from Fort Wallace, from which Pike's Peak could be seen and the range of the Rockies including Long Peak and the mountains back of Denver, when a courier from the post, who had ridden all night, overtook us. . . ."

The day before, messengers from the company suddenly stumbled across two exhausted frontiersmen named Jack Stilwell and Pierre Trudeau.

Stilwell and Trudeau told a harrowing tale of being surrounded on an island with almost fifty other frontiersmen for several days, while Cheyenne and Lakota warriors made repeated charges against them. The warriors were led by Roman Nose.

The scouts were specially recruited by General Sheridan to search out the camps of the Cheyennes and Lakotas and were led by Major George Forsyth.

Some people called them "Forsyth's whiskey

command," because they drank so much. They boasted they could easily rid western Kansas of "renegade Indians," and had scornfully refused an escort of Buffalo Soldiers when they had left Fort Wallace two weeks before.

Now Stilwell and Trudeau begged the messengers to help rescue the command. The soldiers raced to Carpenter's camp at Cheyenne Wells, Colorado, while the frontier scouts hurried to Fort Wallace.

The next morning, Carpenter received orders to use "the greatest despatch" in trying to find and rescue Forsyth's command.

Private Waller and the rest of the men were soon riding north toward lands that were, said Carpenter, "the camping ground and home of the tribes of the Northern Cheyennes and certain affiliated tribes of the Ogallala and Yankton Sioux."

On September 16, a Lakota hunting party had spotted Forsyth's command on the Arikaree, a dry fork of the Republican River, about twenty miles below the camp of Pawnee Killer and his people. Pawnee Killer sent runners to the Cheyennes, asking them to join him in attacking the scouts who had invaded their hunting grounds.

Two Cheyenne chiefs, Tall Bull and White Horse, went to the tepee of Roman Nose and found him undergoing purification ceremonies.

Several days before, he had eaten fried bread that had been cooked by a woman using an iron fork. Roman Nose believed that his ability to escape harm from the white men's bullets required that he not eat anything touched by metal. Only after eating did he find out about the fork, and now he had to purify himself before doing battle again. Tall Bull told him to hurry up, and Roman Nose said he would follow as soon as he could.

The Cheyennes and Lakotas began the fight without him, charging the island where Forsyth and his men had taken cover in tall grass and willow brush. Roman Nose finally came, but stopped his horse atop the high ground overlooking the battle. The warriors quit fighting and waited for him to lead them, but Roman Nose just watched.

Finally, Roman Nose went off to the side and painted himself for battle. He put on his war bonnet of forty crow feathers and rode down to the warriors, who formed a long line behind him. Then he began the charge toward the island.

The horses started out in a slow trot, then raced faster and faster until they were roaring down on the scouts.

Just as he reached the outer edge of the willows, a bullet smashed into Roman Nose's spine. He lay in the brush until dark, then crawled to the bank where some young warriors found him. He died that night.

One historian has written that Roman Nose's death "was like a great light going out in the sky."

Many of the Cheyennes and Lakotas were so grief-
stricken they left the battlefield.

Private Waller and his comrades found their
trail the next day, "in the midst of a wide grass
covered valley." The Buffalo Soldiers also found
five scaffolds on the side of a hill, and on each
scaffold lay the body of a warrior killed by gunshot.

And then, "gazing across the valley, we saw
something white in a ravine on the opposite side,"
reported Carpenter. They hurried to the ravine,
and found that what they'd seen was a tepee built
of freshly tanned skins.

"Inside on a little platform lay the body of an
Indian warrior, evidently a chief or man of con-
sequence, wrapped in buffalo robes," said Carpenter, who didn't realize it was Roman Nose. "An
Indian drum, similar to those used by the Indians
for medicine purposes, a shield and some other
equipments were placed at the head and feet."

It was almost dark, and the cavalrymen camped
for the night.

Early the next morning, before they had time
to saddle up, one of Forsyth's scouts stumbled into
the camp. Following his directions, the soldiers
rode "at a rapid gait for about 18 miles."

Finally, from the top of a hill, they saw "what
appeared to be an island in the midst of the river."
Waller and Carpenter led the charge, and the few
remaining warriors quickly rode away.

"What a sight we saw," said Waller. "Thirty

wounded and dead men right in the midst of fifty dead horses, that had lain in the hot sun for 10 days.

"And these men had eaten the putrid flesh of those dead horses for eight days. The men were in a dying condition when Carpenter and myself dismounted and began to rescue them."

Six of Forsyth's men lay dead. The scouts claimed they'd killed hundreds of warriors, though the Lakotas and Cheyennes later said they lost only about thirty.

But the death of Roman Nose was shattering. The whites called the fight the Battle of Beecher's Island, after Lieutenant Frederick Beecher who died there. The Lakotas and Cheyennes called it the Fight When Roman Nose Was Killed.

Waller said the Buffalo Soldiers buried the dead scouts "with military honors."

The cavalrymen had ridden 100 miles in 26 hours, and almost 500 miles during the month. The warriors that they fought were also riding hard.

Now that Roman Nose was dead, many of the Cheyennes headed south to seek refuge with Black Kettle in Indian Territory. They knew more soldiers would come to hunt them if they stayed in the north, and so they sought survival with their Southern Cheyenne relatives.

Unknown to them, Sheridan was about to begin his winter campaign against Black Kettle and the other chiefs, even though most had kept their treaty obligations.

Black Kettle's village was on the Washita River about one hundred miles west of Fort Cobb, in the southern part of Indian Territory. When the Cheyennes from the north arrived, he scolded the warriors for fighting the soldiers, but welcomed them and their families back.

It had been four years since the groups split apart following the massacre at Sand Creek.

There were many Kiowas and Comanches gathered at Fort Cobb, which the government had designated as the distribution point for supplies promised under the Medicine Lodge Treaty.

In mid-October, Private George Ford and almost one hundred other Buffalo Soldiers arrived at Cobb to help distribute the supplies. They quickly built shelters for themselves and repaired some old buildings to serve as storage places.

Major General William B. Hazen arrived at the fort in early November to talk to the leaders of the Kiowas and Comanches. When he learned that many Cheyennes and Arapahos had camped on the Washita River for the winter, he asked General Sheridan for reinforcements.

When Black Kettle heard about the movements of the soldiers all around him, he rode down the valley of the Washita to talk to Hazen. Little Robe and two Arapaho leaders went with him.

Hazen had commanded Fort Cobb during the

summer, and the Cheyennes and Arapahos enjoyed friendly visits with him. But this time was different.

Black Kettle asked permission to bring his village of 180 lodges nearer Fort Cobb for protection. Hazen, who knew of Sheridan's plans to attack the chief within the next few days, refused.

Hazen said that if the people returned to their villages they would not be attacked.

It was the last week in November 1868.

A tired and discouraged Black Kettle rode back to his village in a driving snowstorm, arriving long after sunset on November 26. He called a council almost as soon as he arrived and told his people they must not be caught by surprise again as they were at Sand Creek.

In the morning, he told them, he would ride out with a delegation to meet the soldiers and talk with them of peace.

The snowstorm continued. A raw wind blew ever colder from the north.

That night Sheridan sent out Custer's cavalry from Camp Supply, telling them to "destroy" the villages of the "savage Indians."

Proceed to the Washita River, Sheridan told Custer, to "the supposed winter seat of the hostile tribes; to destroy their villages and ponies, to kill or hang all warriors, and bring back all women and children."

Black Kettle had risen early the next morning,

as he always did, and stepped out into the fog that covered the Washita. Almost at once he heard a woman yelling, "Soldiers! Soldiers!"

The chief rushed back inside his lodge and grabbed his rifle, then stepped outside and pulled the trigger. The village awoke. His wife untied his pony, brought it to him, and together they raced out to try and talk to the soldiers.

Custer ordered his buglers to play "Gary Owen" as they charged:

> "We'll break windows, we'll break doors,
>   The watch knock down by threes and fours;
> Then let the doctors work their cures,
>   And tinker up our bruises."

Almost at the ford in the Washita, Black Kettle saw the soldiers coming and raised his hand in a gesture of peace. The soldiers shot him down and his wife with him, then splashed over their lifeless bodies and into the village, shooting as they came.

When it was all over, 103 Cheyennes lay dead. All but 11 of them were women, children, and the elderly. Custer also burned their winter meat supply and lodges and slaughtered every one of their several hundred horses.

Back at Camp Supply, Sheridan ordered that Custer and his regiment be greeted with a band and formal review. A few of the Buffalo Soldiers had been stationed at the camp for the campaign and were forced to turn out to watch the grisly parade.

The 7th cavalrymen rode in waving the scalps of Black Kettle and the other dead Cheyennes. In his official report, Sheridan said the army had "wiped out Black Kettle . . . a worn-out and worthless old cipher."

Sheridan claimed he had offered the chief sanctuary if he would come into the fort before the fighting began.

Many white officials who had known Black Kettle bitterly protested the attack on his village, but Sherman gave his wholehearted approval.

"I am well satisfied with Custer's attack," Sherman replied, "and would not have wept if he could have served Satanta's and Bull Bear's band in the same style."

Most of the Buffalo Soldiers knew nothing of this, for they were engaged in their own fight for survival. Their enemy was not the Cheyennes or Arapahos, but the fierce winter weather that struck them on the plains.

The Buffalo Soldiers were the first to take the field in Sheridan's campaign. They set out two weeks before Custer attacked Black Kettle's village, with rations for forty-three days and Wild Bill Hickok as their scout. One company of Custer's cavalry went with them.

On the fifth day out, the men were hit by a heavy snowstorm and bitter cold. They were forced to camp for the night in a desolate area with no wood for fires. The next day they pushed on through heavy snowdrifts.

Twenty-five horses collapsed and had to be shot. The men were forced to walk, and thirty suffered severe frostbite. Their boots fell apart, and the only covering they had for their feet was the hides of dead horses.

Hickok and the Buffalo Soldiers couldn't find the main supply train, and their food began to run out. As the days passed, the soldiers were placed on half-rations and then on one-quarter rations. They were slowly freezing and starving to death.

Finally two of the cavalrymen out searching for the supply train stumbled onto the expedition's chief scout, Buffalo Bill Cody, who was looking for them. It had been six weeks since the Buffalo Soldiers took to the field.

Two days later they joined the rest of the command on the Canadian River, where they remained until they heard the news of Custer's destruction of Black Kettle and his people.

Some of the men decided they'd had enough of army life. On December 5, thirteen of them deserted "in the field in Texas," including a sergeant and a corporal. The harsh conditions they'd just experienced undoubtedly had a lot to do with their actions.

But some of them may have agreed with ex-Sergeant Major Williams, who was already back in civilian life, that "killing people isn't a job for a Christian."

They may also have had second thoughts about what they were doing to Native Americans, because their own relatives were being driven from the land and murdered in the South.

A few weeks before Black Kettle and his people were killed, wrote Williams, "there was a massacre of Colored people" in Louisiana, which "lasted from three to six days, during which time between three and four hundred of them were killed."

The majority of the men who'd started out in the regiment in 1866 and 1867 remained, however, preferring the life they'd found in the army to the life they'd left behind. For every black cavalryman who deserted, ten white ones deserted.

Most of the Buffalo Soldiers of the 10th had hardly been out of the saddle for a year, and now the entire regiment was about to be sent to Indian Territory.

There they would be within striking distance of the Kiowas and Comanches who were raiding Texas settlements.

It was January, the Moon of Strong Cold.

The Moon of Popping Trees

4

The Buffalo Soldiers helped guard and feed the Cheyennes and Arapahos who began surrendering at Fort Cobb at the beginning of 1869.

Sherman said that all who gave up would be fed at the fort as long as they were peaceful, and that all who refused to give up would be killed. Few Kiowas surrendered until Custer, talking to Satanta and Lone Wolf under a flag of truce, suddenly arrested the chiefs. Sherman announced they would be hanged unless their people surrendered, and many of the Kiowas then came in.

Custer and his regiment were sent to round up the Comanches and Kiowas who were still free. The Buffalo Soldiers were glad they didn't have to take to the field, for the weather was almost constantly cold and rainy.

The rains were so torrential at one point that the Washita overflowed and washed some of the men out of their bunks.

There were now four thousand men, women, and children camped around the fort, and Colonel

Grierson described the scene as "lively as well as warlike." Relations were good between the Buffalo Soldiers and the people who had surrendered, because the soldiers spent most of their time passing out food.

Tosawi, a chief of the Comanches, was one of the last to lead his people to the fort.

"Tosawi, good Indian," the old chief said when he was introduced to Sherman.

"The only good Indians I ever saw were dead," Sherman replied. In time, his reply would become the saying: "The only good Indian is a dead Indian."

Sheridan wanted a larger fort built for use in controlling the Kiowas and Comanches and for protecting settlers in Texas. It would also serve as the agency (government administrative center) for the Comanches, Kiowas, and several smaller groups.

The headquarters of the 10th was moved to a location Grierson picked out less than fifty miles north of the Texas border, in the middle of the new Kiowa-Comanche reservation. There the men set up shelter for themselves in tents that had been condemned for use by white troops.

Then the Buffalo Soldiers began building the fort, which was given the temporary name of Camp Wichita because it was on the site of an old Wichita Indian village.

Custer and some of his men were also transferred

to Camp Wichita, but only the Buffalo Soldiers were required to do construction work.

All the Kiowas and Comanches were moved to the area around Camp Wichita, so the Buffalo Soldiers were forced to work on the new fort while also feeding several thousand men, women, and children. The soldiers even had to rebuild the road to the camp and erect a bridge across a creek, so supplies could be brought in.

The men labored through the rest of the winter and into spring. They cut down trees and quarried limestone, which they used in the backbreaking work of building stables, storehouses, living quarters, and a huge stone corral.

Much of the work came to a brief halt when hundreds of Cheyennes and Arapahos streamed in to surrender, after spending the winter in their camps. The men fed them, then took them north almost 150 miles to Camp Supply, which was located on the Cheyenne-Arapaho reservation.

Almost half of the Buffalo Soldiers were stationed at Camp Supply, including Waller and his Company H comrades.

Waller said they built "quarters for men and horses," and had "six thousand Indians on our hands to feed. We had to herd cattle for their beef."

By August, the post was complete enough to give it an official name, Fort Sill, in honor of

Union General Joshua W. Sill, who was killed in the Civil War.

The food and supplies promised by the government continued to be substandard or weren't delivered at all, and soon small groups of warriors were again raiding south into Texas.

For several months, however, the main enemies of the Buffalo Soldiers at both Camp Supply and Fort Sill were white settlers and outlaws. When a gang stole 139 government mules in Indian Territory and headed for Texas, five men from Company H and their lieutenant set out in pursuit.

They rode for two days, finally cornering their quarry in a ravine. In the gun battle that followed, one of the outlaws was killed and the other four captured.

Three confederates of the thieves then showed up for a rendezvous and were also captured. The Buffalo Soldiers returned triumphantly to the fort with 7 prisoners and 127 mules.

The cavalrymen were lucky they were able to complete the chase, for most of them were still riding the "mean and wornout horses of the Seventh Cavalry," complained Captain Carpenter.

"Since our first mount in 1867 this regiment has received nothing but broken down horses and repaired equipment as I am willing to testify to as far as my knowledge goes," he wrote to Grierson.

Grierson repeatedly tried to obtain better horses

and equipment for his men, but was never able to do so.

The men of the 9th were also experiencing the same problems, but with worse consequences. The territory they were assigned to patrol in Texas included thousands of square miles of brush jungle along the Rio Grande and immense areas of desert, plain, and mountain where the going was incredibly rough.

Not only were the men expected to fight Kiowas, Comanches, and Apaches, but they were also given the job of protecting the whole area from Mexican revolutionaries and white outlaws.

The task of the Buffalo Soldiers in the 9th was made even more difficult by the fact that most white Texans hated the sight of black men wearing the uniform of the United States Army.

Many whites had moved to Texas before the Civil War because slavery was legal in the huge territory. By the eve of the Civil War, there were sixty-four counties in Texas that had at least one thousand slaves apiece.

The Texas Rangers were formed partly to recapture escaped slaves who had fled to Mexico, though the escaped slaves more than held their own in battles with the rangers.

Slavery had been abolished less than two years before the men of the 9th rode into the state, and its white citizens were determined to reimpose a system of control over all black people.

The Buffalo Soldiers were thus viewed with intense hostility by most of the people they had come to protect. In the years to come, that hostility would be expressed in many acts of violence.

But in the first few months the men had more pressing problems to deal with.

Emanuel Stance, now a sergeant, was one of the almost one hundred men assigned to Fort Quitman. Quitman was a desolate post on the banks of the Rio Grande opposite the Mexican state of Chihuahua.

It had been established in 1858 to protect the stagecoach and mail lines between San Antonio and El Paso and to guard emigrants on their way to California. The post had been abandoned during the Civil War and, by the time the Buffalo Soldiers arrived, the area was the scene of frequent attacks.

Mescalero Apaches struck the fort twelve times the first month Stance and the other men were there. The soldiers survived the attacks with few casualties, but began to wonder if they could survive the post.

Major Albert P. Morrow, their commander, wrote army officials that most of the buildings "are no longer tenable . . . during heavy rain yesterday, the guardhouse fell in and guard and prisoners narrowly escaped injury . . . houses are not fit to stable cattle in. . . . Quarters have a wagon load of silt on rugs, furniture, etc. . . . The post is a disgrace to the government and a gross injustice to troops to station them there. . . ."

Morrow was told to have his men repair the buildings as best they could, so the soldiers divided their time between construction work and long patrols searching for "hostile Indians."

Sherman visited the fort several months later and called the enlisted men's quarters "hovels in which a negro would hardly go."

The conditions at Quitman, said one of their officers, were simply a reflection of those the Buffalo Soldiers would encounter many times as they were given "the most isolated and undesirable stations in the country. . . ."

The officer complained that the Buffalo Soldiers at Quitman, as well as at all the other posts, were also "required to perform the most abject 'menial labor,' as well as the most arduous campaigning against hostile Indians."

The men at Quitman quickly found out about both the "menial labor" and the "hostile Indians."

The land they had to patrol was remote and sparsely settled. Much of it lay directly astride the "Great Comanche War Trail," the desert route taken by war parties from the north for almost two hundred years on their raids into Mexico.

Two of the first members of the 9th to die in combat were Corporal Samuel Wright and Private Eldridge Jones.

Both had joined up in New Orleans within days

of the government's authorizing formation of the
9th. The twenty-two-year-old Wright was a native
of St. James Parish, Louisiana, and had been a
laborer in civilian life. Jones was a twenty-two-
year-old from Harris County, Georgia, and had
worked as a "steamboatman" before joining the
cavalry.

The two were with a small detachment of Buffalo Soldiers escorting a mail coach on the southern part of the San Antonio-El Paso road, when
they were ambushed and killed.

A few weeks later, more than a hundred Mescalero Apaches attacked a stagecoach being escorted by Buffalo Soldiers east of El Paso. Private
Nathan Johnson was killed. Within days after
that, approximately nine hundred Kickapoos, Lipans, Mexicans, and white outlaws attacked the
men of Company K about seventy-five miles from
Stockton.

The soldiers killed twenty of the attackers in a
three-hour fight, but Privates Andrew Trimble, Eli
Boyer, and William Sharpe were roped and
dragged away. Their bodies were never found.

By the end of 1869, most of the Comanches
and Kiowas had been confined to reservations.
Sheridan released Satanta and Lone Wolf from
arrest at Fort Sill, and the following spring the
Comanches and Kiowas were given permission to
go on a buffalo hunt.

The hunting was good, but the warriors grew

angry when they came across thousands of buffalo carcasses slain by white hunters. The hunters took only the hides and left the meat to rot.

"Has the white man become a child that he should recklessly kill and not eat?" asked Satanta.

Many of the young warriors said they would stay on the plains when winter came and hunt buffalo, rather than return to the reservations and go hungry.

The men of the 9th were about to cross paths with these angry warriors and the men who led them. One of their first encounters was a small one, but it made history: because of his actions in the fight, Emanuel Stance became the first Buffalo Soldier to win the Congressional Medal of Honor.

The sergeant and his command of nine enlisted men were on a scout on the Kickapoo Road near Fort McKavett, searching for two white children who had been kidnapped by warriors.

Suddenly, said Stance, "I discovered a party of Indians making across the hills, having a herd of horses with them. I charged them and after slight skirmishing they abandoned the herd and took to the mountains."

Stance and his men captured the herd, then camped for the night. The next morning, on their way back to the fort, he saw a party of about twenty warriors preparing to attack a small wagon train.

The sergeant led another charge, capturing five

*James P. Beckwourth,
one of the most
famous mountain men.*

*"The Sioux Indians Hunting Buffalo," a painting by George Catlin.
Catlin is under the wolf skin, sketching.*

*Buffalo Soldiers of Troop A, 10th Cavalry,
at Fort Apache, Arizona.*

*A drawing of the Council at Medicine Creek with soldiers of
the U.S. Army and the Kiowa and Comanche Indians.*

Satanta, also known as White Bear, second chief of the Kiowas.

Picture 1-6

*Colonel Benjamin H. Grierson fought hard for equal provisions
and respect for the Buffalo Soldiers.*

Three Cheyenne men.
Left to right: White Antelope, Man on a Cloud, and Roman Nose.

The Issue Room at the Red Cloud Indian Agency,
where Indians received supplies from the government.

*Buffalo Soldier Sgt. Benjamin Brown was assigned
to escort stagecoaches carrying army payroll.*

Quanah Parker and his wife.

Buffalo Soldiers with a scout at Sierra Bonitos, painted by Frederic Remington.

Buffalo Soldiers of the 9th Cavalry in Santa Fe, New Mexico.

Picture 1-10

Picture 1-11

Picture 1-12

George Washington Williams, minister and Buffalo Soldier.

more horses and forcing the warriors to flee with bullets "whistling about their ears." But a short time later he was attacked again as he reached a water hole.

This time, Stance declared, "I turned my little command loose on them at this place, and after a few volleys they left me to continue my search in peace."

Stance eventually found the two children.

When he was presented with the medal a few weeks later, the ex-farmer declared: "I will cherish the gift as a thing of priceless value and endeavor by my future conduct to merit the high honor conferred upon me."

It was now the end of 1870.

The Buffalo Soldiers of the 9th had spent a hard year. Major Albert Morrow, one of their officers, said they had endured "the severest hardships with short rations and no water without a murmur. The negro troops are peculiarly adapted to hunting Indians knowing no fear and capable of great endurance."

The chiefs continued to debate which way to lead their people as the snows piled high across the plains.

Before the winter was over, almost all of them would cross the Red River to raid in Texas. The cavalrymen of the 9th, riding out from six forts stretching almost halfway across the state, were already scouting thousands of square miles of desert and plain as the cold blew ever stronger against the lodges.

When the warriors came, the soldiers would be waiting.

It was December, the Moon of Popping Trees.

The Moon When the Ponies Shed 5

Eighteen-seventy-one was just a few days old when Kiowa and Comanche warriors began raiding Texas.

A large party struck at four men hauling supplies to Fort Griffin on the Butterfield Trail and quickly surrounded them. Griffin was an important supply post for buffalo hunters and settlers, and it provided protection for the trail.

The men slit their horses' throats and used the bodies as a breastwork to hide behind, but were finally killed after a desperate fight.

The last one to die was a man named Brit Johnson, who was known as one of the best shots on the frontier. A rescue party found 173 empty cartridge cases beside his body.

Johnson and his three companions were black. Their deaths were a personal loss to the Buffalo Soldiers, for several had known them. But though the cavalrymen rode long and hard, they could find no trace of the warriors who killed their friends.

A few weeks later, the Texas legislature demanded increased protection from the federal government, claiming that Kiowa, Comanche, and
Apache raids had "not only retarded the settlement of the frontier counties of the State, but have
almost depopulated several counties."

The government sent General Sherman to in-
vestigate. He traveled from fort to fort, escorted
by several Buffalo Soldiers. Sherman said the land
looked good for raising livestock, "as the Indians
are gradually killed off or domesticated."

Unknown to the soldiers or the general, a raiding party that included Satanta, Satank, Big Tree,
and a medicine man named Mamanti the Sky
Walker watched them pass by on the Butterfield
Trail between Forts Richardson and Belknap.

Mamanti the Sky Walker said he had a vision
that they should cross into Texas and drive out
the settlers. Unless that was done, he told the
chiefs, the buffalo would disappear forever.

And so Mamanti and almost one hundred others
in his party watched unseen from a hilltop as the
Buffalo Soldiers and Sherman rode past on the
trail below them. Many of the warriors wanted to
attack, but the medicine man told them a greater
prize would come if they waited.

Since his vision had led to the raid, he was
considered the leader, and they followed his
advice.

Finally the last of the soldiers passed out of sight,

and still the warriors and chiefs waited. The hours went by; then suddenly a wagon train rolled into view. It was headed toward Fort Richardson with supplies for the army.

There were ten wagons and, when they were close enough, Mamanti signaled to Satanta. Satanta raised his bugle to his lips, blew a mighty blast, and the warriors charged. The teamsters formed a circle and fought from behind the wagons, but the raiding party broke through and killed seven of them.

While the rest of the teamsters fled, the warriors searched the wagons. They found nothing but corn. Disgusted, they tied their wounded to horses and rode back north toward the Kiowa-Comanche reservation in Indian Territory and the Buffalo Soldiers who would soon be pursuing them.

The soldiers rode out of Fort Sill and followed what they thought was the trail of the raiders "down through Mexico and back through Colorado and Kansas," said Waller, who was one of the pursuers.

"Old Chief Satank and Santa [Satanta], Lone Wolf and Big Tree, were the chiefs that were at the head of all this. Well, you see they had out-generaled the soldiers and got to Fort Sill five days ahead of us."

Sherman had also left Texas with his escort of Buffalo Soldiers and gone north to Fort Sill, where several hundred members of the 10th were stationed. A few days later, the chiefs came into the fort to draw their rations. The agent in charge of issuing the provisions, a Quaker named Lawrie Tatum, asked if they knew anything about an attack on a wagon train in Texas.

Satanta immediately stepped forward and said he had led the raid, even though he hadn't.

"I have repeatedly asked you for arms and ammunition, which you have not furnished, and made many other requests which have not been granted," Satanta said bitterly. "You do not listen to me talk. The white people are preparing to build a railroad [the Texas and Pacific] through our country, which will not be permitted. . . . On account of these grievances, I took, a short time ago, about one hundred of my warriors, with the chiefs Satank, Eagle Heart, Big Tree, Big Bow, and Fast Bear . . ."

Satank broke in, warning him not to go on, but Satanta ignored him.

"We went to Texas where we captured a train not far from Fort Richardson. . . . Three of our men got killed, but we are willing to call it even. . . . If any other Indian comes here and claims the honor of leading the party he will be lying for I did it myself!"

Tatum hurried to see Grierson and Sherman. The general decided to call the chiefs to a council on the front porch of Grierson's house and arrest them.

Almost two hundred Buffalo Soldiers were ordered to mount up and hide in the stables, so they could be ready to ride and fight. A dozen soldiers crouched behind shuttered windows that opened onto the porch.

Satanta and several of the chiefs came voluntarily, but Satank had to be forced to attend. Big Tree, who had been spotted in the trader's store, refused to come.

A detachment of Buffalo Soldiers was sent to arrest him, and when the chief saw them coming, he threw his blanket over his head and leaped through the glass window. The cavalrymen galloped after him, ran him down in a field, and forced him to surrender.

Sherman told Satanta, Satank, and Big Tree that he was arresting them for killing the teamsters. Satanta shouted that he would rather die than be taken prisoner and reached for a pistol under his blanket.

Sherman gave a command and the twelve soldiers threw open the shutters and leveled their rifles at the chiefs.

Kicking Bird stood up and yelled at Sherman: "You have asked for these men to kill them. But they are my people, and I am not going to let you have them. You and I are going to die right here."

Just then Lone Wolf rode up and walked toward the porch. He threw one of the two carbines he was carrying to one chief and handed his pistol to another, saying in Kiowa: "Make it smoke if any-thing happens."

Then he sat down on the floor opposite Sher-man, staring at him and cocking his remaining carbine. An officer gave an order, and the twelve soldiers drew back the hammers on their rifles.

"No, no, no!" Satanta shouted, throwing up his hands.

A crowd of several hundred Kiowa men, women, and children had gathered across the pa-rade ground in front of Grierson's house, and they yelled in anger when the chiefs were arrested.

Grierson quickly gave a signal and the troopers in the stables came charging out. Over seventy rode to the left of the house, while Waller and forty others rode to the right. Several dozen more lined up in the front and back of the house.

Ten soldiers hurriedly moved into position be-hind the crowd of men, women, and children.

Grierson shouted to his interpreter to tell the Kiowas that violence would not save Satanta and the other chiefs.

The warriors began to move away and were or-dered to halt. Instead, they opened fire with guns and bows and arrows, wounding Private Edward Givins of Company D.

The soldiers fired back, killing one warrior, and hundreds of the Kiowas then raced toward the Wichita Mountains.

Their decision not to try and rescue the chiefs,

declared Waller, "sure saved an awful slaughter for there were two thousand Indians in the camp. Every man, woman and child in the camp was ready to fight, and . . . that would have been one of the greatest massacres in the history of the Indian wars."

Buffalo Soldiers still surrounded Grierson's house.

The colonel told Kicking Bird and the other chiefs that Satanta, Satank, and Big Tree would be held for trial. There was nothing Kicking Bird and the others could do about it, so they reluctantly agreed.

The Buffalo Soldiers then opened ranks, and all but the three arrested chiefs were allowed to return to their people.

Two weeks later, Satanta and Big Tree were forced into one open wagon and Satank into another. All of them were handcuffed and in chains. White cavalrymen under Colonel Ranald Mackenzie's command were assigned to escort them to Jacksboro, Texas, just outside of Fort Richardson.

Satank was chief of an ancient Kiowa military society called the Kaitsenko, the Society of the Ten Bravest, and he began to sing his death song as the wagons rolled out of the fort:

"O sun, you remain forever, but we Kaitsenko must die.

"Oh earth, you remain forever, but we Kait-senko must die."

He called to Satanta and Big Tree: "I am a chief and a warrior, and too old to be treated as a child."

Then he pointed to a tree in the distance and shouted, "I shall never go beyond that tree."

Satank pulled his blanket over his head and gnawed the flesh from his hands. He ripped them through the handcuffs, brought out a concealed knife and leaped up. Before the soldiers could fire, he stabbed one and grabbed the carbine from another.

The soldiers shot him down as he attempted to pull the trigger.

It took an hour for Satank to die. Mackenzie ordered his body thrown into a ditch.

Then the wagon carrying Satanta and Big Tree resumed its journey. It had been two hours since the three were brought out of the guardhouse.

"Two mighty dark hours," Waller remembered years later. "I hate to talk of it."

In July, an all-white jury of ranchers and cow-boys with pistols stuck in their belts began hearing testimony against Satanta and Big Tree in the Jacksboro courthouse.

When the testimony was over, the jurors delib-erated a few minutes, then pronounced the chiefs guilty. The judge promptly sentenced them to be hanged. Many civilians protested, especially Agent Tatum and other Quakers.

The Kiowas were furious when they heard about the verdicts. The governor feared that executing the two would start an all-out war, so he commuted their sentences to life in the state penitentiary.

An angry Sherman declared: "Satanta ought to have been hung, and that would have ended the trouble."

That same month saw Grierson concentrate most of the men of the 10th at Fort Sill, with another two companies at Camp Supply. A detachment of fifty-one men was detailed for escort duty to Albuquerque with an Atlantic and Pacific surveying party, along with two of their officers.

One of the officers was Lieutenant Robert Price, a West Point graduate who had joined the regiment just a few months before. Along the way, Price got into an argument with Privates York Johnson and Charles Smith and shot both men to death.

Price was held in a civilian jail in New Mexico for a few weeks, then released. The army allowed him to resign without further punishment. The Buffalo Soldiers were angry, but there were no incidents.

Throughout the next several months, the soldiers continued to patrol the Red River to prevent raids into Texas. Few warriors tried to cross the boundary, however, and the soldiers turned their attention to white whiskey peddlers and gun runners who had set up their "ranches" on the edge of the Cheyenne-Arapaho reservation.

It was now winter.

The Cheyenne-Arapaho and the Kiowa-Comanche reservations remained fairly quiet throughout the winter.

In the spring, however, Comanche war parties again crossed the Red River to strike at Texas settlers. They were soon joined by Kiowas, who remained angry because of the continued imprisonment of Satanta and Big Tree.

In September 1873, the government brought Satanta and Big Tree to Fort Sill, where the Kiowas thought they would be set free. But Governor Edmund Davis of Texas demanded they be kept in the guardhouse until all the Comanches and Kiowas surrendered their weapons and became farmers.

Lone Wolf and other chiefs rejected these demands and came to a meeting with the governor fully armed, determined to free the chiefs by force if necessary. Warriors took up positions around the guardhouse while the meeting was going on.

The Buffalo Soldiers at Fort Sill saddled up their horses and rode out of the stables, ready to fight.

The government agent in charge of the reservation urged Davis to release the chiefs into his custody, and finally the governor agreed. He warned them, however, that they would be sent to prison again if they left the reservation.

"Whatever the white man thinks best, I want my people to do," Satanta replied.

The fall of 1873 came, and many Kiowas and Comanches made the annual trek to their old hunting grounds on the Texas prairie to kill and dry meat for the winter. But the young warriors again found only bones and rotting carcasses, and when winter came many of the people ate their horses to keep from starving.

Sherman ordered all the warriors and their families to camp within ten miles of Fort Sill and to answer weekly roll calls. He said that all those who did not answer when their names were called, whether they were men, women, or children, would be considered "hostile" and hunted down and killed.

Almost four hundred men of the 10th were transferred to Forts Richardson, Concho, and Griffin in Texas to protect settlers from the trouble that was expected when winter ended.

The soldiers experienced intense hostility from the white settlers, especially in Jacksboro, the northern Texas town where Satanta and Big Tree had been tried and convicted.

Jacksboro had twenty-seven saloons for a population of about two hundred people. Many of the

residents had trailed Satanta and Big Tree toward
Fort Sill after they were released from prison, hop-
ing for a chance to murder them.

Now the settlers let the Buffalo Soldiers of the
10th know they hated black men as much as they
hated Comanches and Kiowas. It was a lesson the
men of the 9th had learned long ago.

In January 1875, Sergeant Edward Troutman
and two privates were charged with murder for
killing one of several cowboys who ambushed their
patrol. Two Buffalo Soldiers were killed in the
ambush. Colonel Edward Hatch and Lieutenant
J. Hansell French were indicted for burglary after
they forced their way into a nearby shack and
retrieved the slain soldiers' uniforms and equipment.

The army refused to help the soldiers defend
themselves, but they borrowed money from comrades, hired a lawyer, and were eventually cleared.

The soldiers also killed four horse thieves and
captured 17 others in the next few months, re-
covering almost 1,200 stolen horses and cattle in
the process.

The attention of the Buffalo Soldiers would
again be focused on the Kiowas and Comanches,
however. White buffalo hunters had worked their
way south from Kansas and Indian Territory,
slaughtering as they came.

In 1871, a tannery in Pennsylvania had discovered that buffalo hides could be used to make com-

mercial leather, so the white hunters killed by the hundreds of thousands and shipped the hides east. When another process was developed to convert the bones into fertilizer or charcoal, entire train loads of buffalo bones also headed east from the praires.

Thousands more buffalo were killed by "sportsmen" as they sat inside railroad carriages crossing the prairie. "Ride the Train and Shoot a Buffalo!" read a typical advertisement from the Kansas Pacific Railroad, which even hired an official taxidermist for its customers.

The Medicine Lodge Treaty barred white hunters from entering the Texas Panhandle, but army officials refused to stop them. From 1872 to 1874, the hunters killed over three and one-half million buffalo.

"Let them kill, skin, and sell until the buffalo is exterminated," declared General Sheridan to a group of protesting citizens, "as it is the only way to bring lasting peace and allow civilization to advance."

In the spring of 1874, the Comanches held a Sun Dance on the reservation. (The Sun Dance was the most important religious ceremony of the year for Native Americans on the Great Plains.) They invited the Kiowas to attend and decide what action should be taken against the hunters.

Quanah Parker led his Kwahadi Comanches in from the Staked Plains and said the stench of rotting buffalo filled the air. A Kwahadi prophet named Isatai said only war would save the buffalo.

Lone Wolf, who attended the ceremony with Satanta, also spoke for war. Texans had killed his son and nephew a few weeks before, and Buffalo Soldiers pursued the grieving chief when he tried to bring their bodies home for burial.

Now Lone Wolf wanted to go back to Texas and fight.

Satanta and the young men who followed him also volunteered to fight. Altogether seven hundred warriors agreed to try and drive out the hated hunters once and for all. The chiefs and warriors chose Quanah Parker to lead them.

Most of the Buffalo Soldiers were now deployed in Texas or in Indian Territory close to the Texas border, in preparation for what seemed almost certain war.

The Buffalo Soldiers, said Waller, had already been "almost two years in the cavalry saddle."

Army leaders made plans to carry the war into the heartland of Quanah Parker and his people, where the Comanches and Kiowas still found refuge.

Sergeant Jacob Wilks of the 9th's Company I helped ready his men for the coming expedition. The sergeants of other companies did the same.

Their goal, declared Wilks, would be "the destruction of several Indian villages far out on the Staked Plains."

The Red River War of 1874–75 was about to begin, and hundreds of warriors would strike the first blow.

A suffocating heat spread over the Great Plains, drying up water holes and streams. Great clouds of grasshoppers invaded the land, stripping much of the vegetation bare. A train in Nebraska was forced to a halt when it ran into three-foot-high drifts of grasshoppers.

Nature itself seemed to reflect the anger of men as they rode over the stone-hard earth.

It was May, the Moon When the Ponies Shed.

The Hot Weather Begins Moon

6

The sweltering summer had barely begun when war parties struck across the southern plains.

The Buffalo Soldiers practically lived in their saddles, racing throughout northern and western Texas, Indian Territory, and Kansas after warriors who killed settlers, burned ranches, and ambushed stagecoaches.

White buffalo hunters were the warriors' special targets, and they tried to kill them wherever they found them.

At dawn on June 27, 1874, Quanah Parker and his force of Cheyennes, Kiowas, Comanches, and Apaches attacked the buffalo hunters' base in the Texas Panhandle, a trading post called Adobe Walls.

Quanah led several thundering charges, but the hunters were well barricaded and had telescopic sights on their rifles. They shot one warrior off his horse at a distance of a mile.

The warriors were never able to break into the

post, and by the time Quanah called off the attack, fifteen of his men were dead and many lay wounded. Only three of the twenty-eight hunters were killed.

The hunters said the warriors' attack, which lasted almost all day, was "directed by bugle calls until their bugler was killed late in the afternoon."

The body of a black man was found on the battlefield, with a bugle beside him. He was thought to be a soldier who had deserted, but no one could identify him.

The hunters cut off the heads of the dead warriors and the black man and stuck them on fence posts.

The fires of the Red River War burned faster and faster.

By midsummer, 1,800 Cheyennes, 2,000 Comanches, and 1,000 Kiowas had left the reservations to camp along the various forks of the Red River in the Texas Panhandle. It was remote country where they had always been safe.

But now five columns of soldiers began to converge on them from north, south, east, and west.

Many of the people who fled the reservations camped in or near a place most white men didn't even know existed: Palo Duro Canyon, the Place of Chinaberry Trees. The last great herd of buffalo on the southern plains, like the warriors who hunted them, also sought refuge in the canyon.

General Sherman ordered the troops to pursue the Kiowas, Comanches, and Cheyennes until they surrendered or were killed.

"The more we can kill this year, the less will have to be killed the next war," he said shortly after coming to the West, "for the more I see of these Indians the more convinced I am that they all have to be killed or be maintained as a species of paupers."

The columns totaled three thousand cavalrymen and infantrymen, plus Tonkawa, Navajo, and Seminole-Negro scouts. Each column had several pieces of heavy artillery, though those belonging to the Buffalo Soldiers were so old the officers feared they would explode if fired more than once.

Sergeant Wilks and the Buffalo Soldiers with him traveled northwest from Fort Concho, toward thousands of square miles of land so barren it was still largely unknown to all but Native Americans. The scouts and white soldiers went with them.

The march in the relentless heat, said Wilks, was "long and weary." The soldiers traveled for a month before discovering a hidden village near Palo Duro Canyon.

They waited all night, then charged at dawn.

The surprised warriors somehow managed to hold them off long enough for the women and children to escape, but the fleeing people could carry nothing with them.

"We destroyed everything destructive in their

village," said Wilks. "They had many guns, mostly citizens' rifles, and a good supply of ammunition besides bows, arrows, quivers, lances, etc. These we destroyed. We found a vast amount of buffalo robes, of which each man made choice of the best — the rest were destroyed.

"Their tents were made of poles over which hides were stretched, and these were all burned. We also captured a vast store of dried turkey and buffalo meat; also a considerable amount of peculiar food made in the form of a paste from mesquite beans and other ingredients and put up in the maw of deer and buffalo. . . .

"We captured 112 prisoners, mostly women, children, old 'bucks,' and three or four of the younger warriors. They were brought to Fort Concho and held six or eight months and finally taken to the Fort Sill reservation. While on the march to Fort Concho, three of the younger 'bucks' committed suicide by butting out their brains, preferring a violent death to captivity."

Officers ordered the soldiers to round up all the horses they could find and drive them into a valley to be killed. The soldiers rounded up the two thousand horses, picked out the best ones for themselves, and shot the rest.

Buzzards were circling the valley when the soldiers rode away.

The Buffalo Soldiers of the 10th left Fort Sill in the last column to take the field, riding west into Texas toward the headwaters and tributaries of the Red River. Their mission was to try and drive any warriors they could find into the path of the other four columns.

The dry, torrid weather suddenly turned so wet that streams rose to the tops of their banks and the prairie turned to mud. The fleeing warriors later called their pursuit by the soldiers "the wrinkled-hand chase."

The five columns of soldiers crossed and re-crossed the plains, drawing the noose over tighter around the Kiowas, Comanches, and Southern Cheyennes who had fled the reservations.

More and more men, women, and children were caught or were forced to surrender because of ex-haustion, hunger, and pain.

By the end of September, the men of the 10th had ridden a total of almost three thousand miles.

The cavalrymen in the 9th's Company K were some of the busiest in the expedition. They scouted parts of the Salt Fork, Canadian, and North Fork rivers in the Texas Panhandle and then rode into the Staked Plains for a total dis-tance covered in October of "one Thousand miles more or less."

It had been hot when the expedition began; then it had become wet. Now, without warning, cold and bitter blizzards descended on the men.

In November, a detachment of Buffalo Soldiers under Lieutenant Colonel George Buell was scouting toward the headwaters of the Red River when they suddenly ran into what Buell called "as severe weather as I have ever experienced."

The men were forced to go into camp for several days. They struggled desperately to survive as the winds howled all around them. Almost as soon as they resumed their march, they found and burned a village of twenty-two deserted lodges.

The soldiers also found a supply of horse meat and realized with a shock that the men, women, and children they were chasing were now eating their horses to stay alive.

Other soldiers were finding similar signs of desperation. They began to capture the wounded who could be carried no further. Next they began to catch the elderly, women, children, and, finally, the warriors.

The warriors had been forced to travel and fight while trying to protect their families and live off an increasingly hostile land. They lived in constant fear, never knowing when the soldiers would come crashing into their camps.

The soldiers had only themselves to worry about, and they were supplied by wagons filled with provisions. But they, too, were reaching the end of their endurance as the miles passed by in a numbing blur of cold and exhaustion.

The Buffalo Soldiers under Buell found themselves riding into a blinding snowstorm that whipped their eyes and lashed their hands. They hunched over their exhausted horses as the snow changed to pouring rain and sleet that stung their skin through the lightweight clothing they still wore.

Many of the men watched helplessly as their boots fell apart.

Still the soldiers pushed on, but soon found themselves riding into a raging blizzard. The water froze in their canteens, and many of the men lost all feeling in their fingers and toes. At last Buell ordered the column to turn around and head for the protection of Fort Griffin.

"I cannot give them too much credit for manly endurance without complaint," Buell said of the soldiers under his command.

The Buffalo Soldiers under Lieutenant Colonel John Davidson also ran into bitter cold. More than two dozen troopers suffered severe frostbite, one hundred of their horses dropped dead, and food for men and animals was almost gone.

Davidson finally turned his men toward Fort Sill. Though there were still small parties of Kiowas, Cheyennes, and Comanches out on the plains, for all practical purposes the Red River War was over.

The Buffalo Soldiers had ridden more miles, captured more people, and destroyed more lodges than any other regiments in the war.

Sherman ordered the arrest of all chiefs and warriors suspected of being "ringleaders" in the flight from the reservations. His old enemy, Satanta, was number one on the list.

Satanta and Big Tree had fled their village near Fort Sill with over 160 men, women, and children when the war began. They took no part in the fighting, but were afraid to come back to the fort.

Finally they voluntarily surrendered. Satanta and Big Tree protested their innocence, but were shackled and thrown into the guardhouse.

"No evidence has reached this office of any hostility on their part," protested the superintendent of the plains tribes, Enoch Hoag, in urging freedom for Satanta and Big Tree.

Sherman didn't care about Big Tree, who was soon released, but a shackled Satanta was handed back to the Texans who hated him and his people, to spend the rest of his life behind bars.

Military authorities demanded that Kicking Bird choose 26 Kiowas to be sent to a military prison in Saint Augustine, Florida. Kicking Bird reluctantly agreed, choosing Lone Wolf, Mamanti the Sky Walker, White Horse, Woman's Heart, and 22 young warriors and Mexican captives who had grown up with the Kiowas.

The authorities also singled out several other chiefs for arrest, including Black Horse of the Comanches and Medicine Water, Gray Beard, and Minimic of the Cheyennes.

Several of the black cavalrymen were ordered to arrest Cheyenne warriors and guard them until they could be shipped to the prison in Florida.

All went smoothly until a blacksmith began to put shackles on one of the men. Some Cheyenne women standing nearby taunted him as a coward for standing by quietly while the blacksmith bound him.

The warrior listened in silence for a few moments, then suddenly knocked over the blacksmith and ran for the Cheyenne camp. The soldiers shot and killed him, but many of their bullets hit the lodges in the camp.

The Cheyennes responded with arrows, then fled to a sand hill where they dug up arms and ammunition they'd buried before surrendering.

The colonel in charge of the post ordered the Buffalo Soldiers and members of the 6th Cavalry to drive the Cheyennes from the hill. It was crowded with between 100 and 150 warriors, with women and children behind them.

"We charged them," said Corporal George Berry of Company M. "While rolling around on the ground . . . my rifle got some sand in the breech. I had to take a stick to clean it out, and in doing so I got shot in the right side. I laid down behind a stump, and again those Indians fired a number of shots, but none of them hit me. Some came so close to me that they threw sand in my face."

The soldiers killed two Cheyennes, but attempts to charge the hill were driven back by accurate gunfire. Ten of the Buffalo Soldiers were wounded and one, Private Clark Young, was killed. Five of the white cavalrymen were wounded, but most of the wounds were slight.

The soldiers stayed at the foot of the hill all night, and at daylight discovered that it was deserted. They chased the fleeing Cheyennes for almost 400 miles, but failed to catch them.

There was nowhere for the warriors and their families to hide, however, and by the end of the month all but a handful had returned.

The officers of the white cavalry regiment blamed the Buffalo Soldiers and one of their officers for the failure to dislodge the Cheyennes from the hill.

Another officer in the 10th, Second Lieutenant Edward Turner, said his men were a bunch of "goddamned Moacks who wouldn't fight."

The calvarymen and the other officers of the 10th were outraged, and Grierson wanted Turner court-martialed in justice to the soldiers. The army denied his request and, as so often happened, the official report of the incident contained praise only for the white soldiers.

Seventy-four prisoners were shackled and chained, then taken to the railroad amid the wailing of grief-stricken women. Sergeant Isam Malry joined seven other Buffalo Soldiers and one officer as guards on the journey to the ancient Spanish fortress that would serve as their prison.

It must have been as strange a trip for the Buffalo Soldiers as for the prisoners and, in some ways, as depressing.

They were traveling across lands where the state and federal governments often refused to protect the lives of their own relatives, and where the soldiers themselves were in danger because of the color of their skin.

Sergeant Malry and his men completed their strange journey, then returned to the West to fight more Native Americans.

So much had changed since the soldiers first rode into the plains eight years before, and one incident showed that change more starkly than almost anything else could have: as the last of the Buffalo Soldiers were leaving Indian Territory to join their comrades in Texas, Quanah Parker was leaving Texas to take the last of his followers into Fort Sill.

All winter he and the Kwahadis had fled deeper and deeper into the Staked Plains, changing camp every day as they fled the soldiers. The Kwahadis' horses were exhausted, their equipment was falling apart, and sometimes their only food was grubs and field mice.

Army scouts found them and said they would be annihilated before the summer was over if they didn't surrender.

At the time of the Medicine Lodge Treaty in

1867, Quanah Parker told a friend that his people would never "live on a reservation. Let the white chiefs know that the Kwahadis are warriors. We'll surrender when the blue-coats come and whip us on the Staked Plains."

Now his people could resist no longer, so Quanah Parker finally surrendered. The destruction of the buffalo and the relentless pursuit of the soldiers, had compelled chiefs all across the southern plains to bring their people into the forts. Quanah Parker was the last.

For hundreds of years the Comanches had been unsurpassed as horsemen, free to roam when and where they pleased and to hunt the buffalo that gave them life. Now most of the buffalo on the southern plains were dead (the last four would be tracked down and killed by white hunters on the Staked Plains in 1889), and the Kwahadis were "prisoners of war."

A centuries-old way of life thus came to an end on a warm summer day in 1875.

With the last of the Buffalo Soldiers crossing the Red River into Texas, all the men of the 9th and 10th were now serving in the same military department for the first time.

Soon many of them would come to know the land that Quanah Parker and the Comanches had known, especially the barren heart of the Staked Plains.

The soldiers' journeys into this mysterious and dangerous place would be looked at with awe a century later. Some of the men would die as they rode beneath a scorching sun into a wind that burned as if it came from a giant furnace.

It was June, the Hot Weather Begins Moon.

The Moon of the Red Blooming Lilies

7

Great cattle trails now led north from Texas up through the old Kiowa and Comanche hunting grounds.

The trails snaked a thousand miles and more to the new towns springing up along the railroads: Dodge City and Abilene, Kansas; Cheyenne and Laramie, Wyoming; Ogallala and Sidney, Nebraska; Glendive and Miles City, Montana.

The golden era of the cowboy had begun, and the Buffalo Soldiers helped make it possible. It is estimated that five thousand black cowboys joined fifteen thousand white ones in the "long drives" to the railroads.

White settlers wanted to expand cattle raising into the western part of the state, but a few Kiowas, Lipans, Comanches, and Apaches still fought back.

Mexican revolutionaries crossed the Rio Grande to raid for money and supplies. Texas authorities published a list of five thousand wanted men, and there were so many stagecoach robberies that one man predicted, "It will not be long before stage-robbing will be one of the recognized industries of the country."

The men of the 9th were soon transferred to New Mexico, so the Buffalo Soldiers of the 10th were forced to patrol tens of thousands of square miles in Texas by themselves.

Unknown to the soldiers, they were about to undertake one of the most arduous expeditions in the history of the United States Army in the West.

The Staked Plains, or Llano Estacado as the Spanish called the 90,000 square miles in north-western Texas, was still unsettled by whites.

Although Quanah Parker and most of his fol-lowers were penned up on the reservation at Fort Sill, several Apaches had joined runaway Coman-che warriors in secret hiding places on the plains.

And while soldiers under Mackenzie and others had penetrated limited parts of the area, most whites still looked on the Staked Plains with fear and awe. To them, and to the government, it remained an unknown country filled with hidden danger.

The Buffalo Soldiers were assigned the task of removing the danger and mapping the country for the first time, so that white settlers could finally move into western Texas and eastern New Mex-ico.

The Staked Plains, wrote a rare traveler in 1832,

presented a scene of "barren monotony and desolation."

The plains were higher than the surrounding country, rising in places to 4,500 feet, and they stretched from the Texas Panhandle west into New Mexico. There was nothing to see but sand, windswept grass, and the horizon. In early spring and late fall the temperatures often rose or fell precipitously.

Many early travelers — including the Spanish explorer Coronado, who crossed the plains in 1541 — found it almost impossible to keep from getting lost in the vast, treeless reaches. And so they "staked" the trail with piles of bones and buffalo skulls, giving the area its name.

Lieutenant Colonel William Shafter, commander of the all-black 24th Infantry, was chosen to lead the scouting expedition. Grierson was angry that he wasn't given command, but Shafter was an experienced frontiersman.

His orders were to pursue "hostile Indians" and to "show in detail, the resources of the country passed over, looking to its adaptability for cultivation and stock-raising."

Shafter was ordered to pay special attention to locating sources of water, so that settlers would know where to build towns and obtain water for their journeys further west.

The expedition set out from Fort Concho in the

summer of 1875. The temperature was over 100°
Fahrenheit. It was the kind of weather that once
led General Sheridan to remark that "if I owned
hell and Texas, I'd rent out Texas and live in hell."

The cavalrymen were still riding horses used up
or rejected by the white regiments and, in spite
of the heat, were dressed in the army's regulation
all-wool uniforms.

All the soldiers in the expeditionary force were
black. Most of the companies were undermanned,
so the total number of soldiers was only about four
hundred.

The expedition was guided by Tonkawa and
Seminole-Negro scouts. The Seminole-Negro
scouts, though never numbering more than about
thirty at any one time, earned a reputation as being
among the most effective units ever to serve in
the army.

These men of mixed black and Seminole heritage signed on with the army because they were
destitute and were promised land for their families.
It was a promise the U.S. Government never kept.

Now the scouts and soldiers moved out on an
expedition that would last six months and change
the future of that part of the Southwest.

The Buffalo Soldiers, like Coronado and his
men before them, were about to discover the un-
forgiving harshness of the land.

The first hint of the ordeal to come was in August, when the men of the 10th covered a total

of almost three thousand miles. They marched "over the Staked Plains . . . [men] and horses suffered severely from the want of water." One stretch of land was so rough they had to dismount and lead their horses seventy-seven miles in order to reach the supply camp.

September and October were even worse, with several troopers being forced to abandon their exhausted horses or shoot them "for Mercy."

The soldiers moved through what must have seemed a constant haze of thirst and exhaustion until finally, in late November, the first of them reached the safety of Fort Concho.

Two weeks later, the last members of the expedition rode into Fort McKavett "after an absence of six months and seven days."

The Buffalo Soldiers had scouted almost ten thousand miles over incredibly rough terrain and had endured some of the harshest weather conditions in the United States.

They had found and marked almost every source of water on the Staked Plains. On a hill near one large spring, beside a hastily abandoned camp of several lodges, the soldiers erected a seven-and-one-half-foot stone marker that could be seen from miles away. For years afterwards, the marker guided thirsty settlers to the lifesaving water at "Monument Spring."

Most of the scouting was through country that had never been seen before by soldiers of the

United States Army. Soon ranchers and home-steaders, armed with knowledge gained by the expedition, began taking possession of what had been the last great home of the southern plains Native Americans.

The Buffalo Soldiers, for better or worse, had helped make it possible. But Shafter's voluminous official reports never even mentioned them.

Unfortunately for some of the Buffalo Soldiers, they would have to venture onto the Staked Plains again. This time conditions would be even worse than the ones they had already encountered, and several of the men would die.

Their ordeal, which would become famous throughout the United States, began in the spring of 1877 when Black Horse led a large band of Comanche warriors off the reservation at Fort Sill and into the Staked Plains. At the same time, Mescalero Apaches were raiding along the San Antonio-El Paso road and into the Guadalupe Mountains of western Texas and eastern New Mexico.

Sergeant Joseph Claggett rode after them with a detachment of Buffalo Soldiers, but had to stop when eight of their horses dropped dead from exhaustion.

Grierson then ordered Private Barney Howard and thirty-nine other men, with Captain Nicholas Nolan in command, to ride into the plains "after hostile Indians and for the protection of settlers."

Lieutenant Charles Cooper was second in command. Most of the cavalrymen were raw recruits who had just arrived at Fort Concho.

They set out in searing heat.

There had been a drought all year, but at first, water was no problem. The men set up a supply camp, and twenty of them were left behind to guard it. The rest of the company, joined by almost two dozen buffalo hunters and a Mexican guide, tried to track down the warriors.

Two days after starting out, the soldiers and hunters intercepted Quanah Parker and several of his followers.

Nolan wanted to arrest the chief, who was "liberally supplied with Government Horses, Equipments, Arms, Ammunition and Rations."

But Parker produced a pass from army authorities saying he had been sent out to persuade runaways to return to Fort Sill, and Nolan reluctantly let him go.

The men pushed on to a water supply found by the soldiers under Shafter two years before. Now, however, the ground was dry and hard.

Nolan reported that the command "was compelled to dig several holes and dip out the water with small tin cups. . . . This was a long and tedious job."

The soldiers resumed their quest, traveling forty miles over the next two days. At each place where they expected to find water, they found only dry earth. The guide and several of the hunters finally struck out on their own to search, while the soldiers stayed in camp.

Nolan and the Buffalo Soldiers followed the next day, finding the guide and hunters seventeen miles away at a place called Dry Lake.

"At this place no water could be found either for men or Horses," Nolan said.

The men of the command now began a frantic search. The guide said there was water due west not more than fifteen or twenty miles away, so the men rode until it was too dark to see the trail. They saddled up again at dawn and rode for about fifteen miles.

Their tongues were swollen and their throats were so dry they couldn't swallow food. Some of them tried to eat brown sugar, but their parched mouths wouldn't even allow the sugar to dissolve.

The going was increasingly slow because many of the men were so faint they kept falling off their horses.

"We were now in the sand hills," Nolan reported. "The Command now commenced to suffer exceedingly for water. . . . Up to this time I had three men sun struck. . . . We had marched about fifty-five miles under a broiling sun over a barren sandy plain without a drop of water."

Nolan gave all the canteens to eight "old soldiers" and told them to follow the guide, who had pushed on ahead.

The next day the command marched fifteen miles, but found no trace of the guide or of the eight soldiers. Nolan concluded that the guide, "as well as all of us, was lost on the Staked Plains, without water and no prospects of getting any. . . ."

Men and horses were now staggering all around. The men felt an overwhelming sense of suffocation because of the swelling in their throats. They became suspicious of each other and had trouble seeing and speaking.

"If this keeps up much longer," Nolan said late in the afternoon, "we will each be dethroned of his reason, and be a wandering lot of maniacs until a merciful death relieves us."

When one of the horses staggered and fell, Lieutenant Cooper "had his throat cut, and the blood distributed amongst them. The captain and I drank heartily of the steaming blood. . . ."

Men and officers then "laid down on the open prairie and endeavored to obtain such shelter from the fearful heat as a woolen blanket thrown over a small mesquite bush would afford. This, our fourth day without water, was dreadful. . . ."

Private Howard somehow found the strength to go from man to man, cheering them with amusing stories and reminding Lieutenant Cooper of the wife waiting for him back at Fort Concho.

At twilight, Nolan told the men to abandon all their food and excess equipment, in a last desperate effort to survive. Then the lost patrol began its final march.

Nolan and Cooper led the way astride two mules, for the two horses apiece they had started out with were dead.

It was like a scene from a nightmare. The command, said Nolan, now consisted almost solely of "madmen" whose minds had given way.

"Men gasping in death around us," remembered Cooper of the march, "horses falling dead to the right and left; the crazed survivors of our men fighting each his neighbor for the blood of the horses as the animals' throats were cut. Prayers, curses, and howls of anguish intermingled came to one's ears from every direction. There was rain, apparently, in the far-away distance, yet never a drop for us."

They marched from 8 P.M. to 3 A.M., when suddenly they came across an old wagon trail and followed it to a lake filled with water glistening in the moonlight.

"Such wild hurrahs and firing of guns you never heard in your life," Cooper wrote his father.

At last the ordeal was over. The men had marched over four hundred miles in eighty-six hours without a drop of water.

Four of the soldiers were dead: Privates John T. Gordon, Isaac Derwin, John Isaacs, and John Bond. All four died shortly before water was found.

Four men were later charged with desertion and

sentenced to a year in prison. But the conduct of most of the men, declared Nolan, "was exemplary."

The cavalrymen rested briefly, then joined other Buffalo Soldiers from the 9th and 10th in pursuit of "hostile Apaches" down trails no other soldiers had traveled.

The struggle would last for years and rage from the rocky vastnesses of the Guadalupe Mountains in Mexico and Texas, to the deserts and mountains of Arizona, to the badlands bordering the upper Rio Grande in New Mexico.

The Apaches had been fighting to keep their land for three hundred years — first against the Spanish, then against the Texans, and finally against the soldiers of the United States Army.

Their most famous chief, Cochise, was dead. But they now had a leader who would go down in history as the embodiment of fierce resistance and determination to be free. He was not a chief, but a highly respected warrior and medicine man. His people called him by the name he had been given as an easygoing child, Goyathlay — One Who Yawns — but the Buffalo Soldiers would come to know him by the name they heard whites use: Geronimo.

It was July, the Moon of the Red Blooming Lilies.

The Moon of Deer Horns Dropping Off —— 8

While the Buffalo Soldiers of the 10th were busy protecting Texas settlers and scouting the Staked Plains, those in the 9th were given the task of tracking down Apaches found off their reservations in New Mexico.

It was a task both the soldiers and their commander, Colonel Edward Hatch, heartily disliked. As usual, the government failed to deliver much of the promised food and other supplies, and the Apaches often went hungry.

If they left the reservations to hunt, an angry Hatch wrote General Sheridan, the soldiers had orders to kill them. But if the Apaches stayed on the reservations and tried to live off the government food, they would starve.

Sheridan turned a deaf ear to Hatch's complaint, and the men of the 9th spent long, weary hours chasing small raiding parties led by Juh and Geronimo. In 1876 alone, the Buffalo Soldiers rode almost nine thousand miles in New Mexico.

The Apaches grew angrier as white settlers invaded the reservations and stole horses or tried to stake out homesteads on some of the best reservation land.

The Buffalo Soldiers caught several of the white rustlers and forcibly evicted many of the illegal squatters. But there were always more, and soon revenge-seeking Apache war parties were striking at isolated ranches throughout southern Arizona and New Mexico.

In January 1877, a small detachment of Buffalo Soldiers left Fort Bayard in southwestern New Mexico. Accompanied by Navajo scouts and Lieutenant Henry Wright, they searched for a group that had clashed with soldiers just over the Arizona border.

The soldiers caught up with the party of about fifty Apache men, women, and children, and Wright tried to talk them into surrendering. The warriors refused, saying that if they gave up their guns, only the *waisichu* ("black white men") would have guns.

The warriors quickly surrounded the soldiers, and a fight broke out. Corporal Clinton Greaves and his companions opened fire, killing two warriors. The remainder retreated "to the surrounding cliffs and rocks from where they opened a hot fire."

The position of the soldiers and scouts, said one man, was "much exposed and untenable." The soldiers ran out of ammunition and had to fight hand-to-hand, using their guns as clubs.

They would have been overwhelmed, declared Wright, but for the actions of Corporal Greaves, "who fought like a cornered lion and managed to shoot and bash a gap through the swarming Apaches, permitting his companions to break free."

The conduct of the soldiers was described by the Fort Bayard commander as "deserving of the highest praise" and as "an example of gallantry and soldierly conduct worthy of emulation by all."

Corporal Greaves was singled out "for coolness and courage" and awarded the Congressional Medal of Honor.

The leader of the Apaches the soldiers clashed with was said to be Chief Victorio, a man the Buffalo Soldiers would come to know all too well.

Speculators from Tucson, a town of a few thousand gamblers, saloon keepers, miners, government contractors, and settlers, wanted the land the Apaches lived on because much of it contained good supplies of water and timber.

The speculators were politically powerful, and in a few weeks orders came from Washington for all Apaches to be removed to a barren reservation in eastern Arizona called White Mountain.

One general called the removal "a harsh and cruel measure." Other officers warned that the move would lead to warfare, but the politicians ignored them.

Victorio and Geronimo were told by Apache

scouts that the authorities wnted to speak to them. When the two leaders showed up, they were arrested, shackled, and placed in wagons for the journey to San Carlos (the agency for White Mountain).

A week later, a handful of Buffalo Soldiers joined more than twenty scouts in forcing the followers of Geronimo and Victorio to leave the mountains they loved for the desolation of San Carlos. White settlers fired on the Apaches along the way.

Victorio broke out a few weeks after arriving at the place one man called "Hell's Forty Acres," and the Buffalo Soldiers raced after him.

During the chase, Corporal James Betters was accidentally shot by a sergeant.

While Betters lay dying, he asked to be buried in the cemetery at Fort Bayard. His company commander promised that his wish would be granted.

Betters's body was interred in the cemetery, but in such a way that his comrades and Captain Charles Beyer, the company commander, were outraged. The corporal's face wasn't even washed, and a convict drove the body to the cemetery in a garbage cart.

Betters was "a soldier who had served his country honestly and faithfully for eleven years," an angry Beyers wrote to the adjutant general. Yet he was taken to the cemetery "without a flag covering his coffin, without a formal escort, without a single mourner or friend to follow the poor fellow's remains to their last resting place."

The army ordered an investigation, but no charges were brought.

Victorio soon surrendered and was allowed to return to his old reservation with his followers. A few months later, however, he fled again when the army ordered their return to San Carlos. Victorio stayed out a few weeks, then surrendered again.

It would be the last time.

Victorio and his people were sent over one hundred miles east to a reservation near Fort Stanton, a post established to help control Apaches in south-central New Mexico.

The soldiers were kept busy protecting Apaches from roving gangs of white outlaws who rode onto the reservation to kill and steal, but the Apaches themselves were quiet.

All of that changed suddenly in the summer of 1879, however, when a judge and district attorney appeared on the reservation.

Victorio, fearing he would be arrested on old charges of horse stealing and murder, fled south. He hid in the mountains of Mexico and began to recruit warriors, vowing to "make war forever" on the United States.

Victorio's War, the bloodiest chapter in the history of New Mexico, was about to begin.

The Buffalo Soldiers stationed at Ojo Caliente

(Warm Springs), the home Victorio had never wanted to leave, would be the first to feel his wrath.

The men of the 9th's Company E were commanded by Captain Theodore Hooker, and for years they had complained about his racially derogatory comments and actions. They said he regularly cursed them and called them "god damn dirty niggers" and "baboons."

Hooker once handcuffed a trooper to a wagon and forced him to walk beside it for five days.

Rumors came to the men and officers at Ojo Caliente that Victorio was in the vicinity. In spite of the rumor, Hooker reduced the guard on the herd of horses from eight men to five, and armed them with pistols instead of the more effective carbines.

The guards were in command of Sergeant Silas Chapman.

When their comrades complained that their friends had been placed in a potentially deadly situation, Hooker refused to change his orders.

Victorio and his warriors struck the horse herd on September 4, 1879. Within minutes, forty-six of the company's fifty horses had been run off and the guards lay dead: Sergeant Chapman and Privates Lafayette Hoke, William Murphy, Silas Graddon, and Alvrew Percival.

A Texas Ranger who arrived on the scene shortly after the raid said that the Apaches took "stake-pins made of iron and about twenty inches long . . . and drove one through each soldier's corpse, pinning it firmly to the earth."

The other soldiers charged that after Victorio's raid, Hooker said he wished all of them had been killed and he would do his best to see they were.

The captain blamed the complaints of racism on a Private Nance, "a champion of his race" and "esteemed to be something of an oracle in the Co."

The army ordered an investigation of Hooker and agreed that many of the men's charges were true, but took no disciplinary action against him.

Victorio's attack at Ojo Caliente marked the beginning of one of the hardest campaigns in the history of the United States Cavalry.

Other groups of Apaches joined the fighting. A black man described as a "renegade Negro," presumably a deserter from the army, fought alongside Bonito and other warriors from White Mountain in attacks on settlers in southern New Mexico.

Over the next several months, the Buffalo Soldiers rode thousands of miles, usually just a step behind Victorio and his followers.

"Victorio's capture is not very probable," said General John Pope, commander of the Department of New Mexico, "but the killing (cruel as it will be) can, I suppose, be done in time."

Every company of the 9th was thrown into the field, along with Apache and Navajo scouts.

Less than two weeks after Victorio's raid at Ojo

Caliente, Buffalo Soldiers and Navajo scouts caught up with him shortly after daybreak in a canyon in the Black Range Mountains of western New Mexico. The soldiers thought they had him trapped, but Victorio and his warriors were strongly entrenched on the cliff sides and fired down from behind boulders.

"The Indians are thoroughly armed and abundantly supplied with ammunition," Colonel Hatch reported earlier. "Their fire in action is incessant. . . ."

It was no different this time, and the soldiers were subjected to a "constant fire which lasted all day."

The Buffalo Soldiers, said one of their officers, "made attack after attack to turn the flank of the Indians," but each attack was "as frequently repulsed, with loss, due to the precipitous nature of the country."

By sundown, five of the soldiers lay dead, and many more were wounded. They were left with only a few rounds of ammunition apiece, and their commander ordered a retreat "in the twilight under cover of three volleys."

The men sprinted across the rocky ground to the safety of a hill to make their last stand, but one wounded man was left behind.

From where the man was lying to the safety of the hill "was about 400 yards, all open to fire from the rocky crest of the ridge where the Indians in overwhelming force were fighting."

The wounded man tried to walk, but couldn't.

"The fire of the hostiles increased so much," said the officer, "that it seemed as if no one could pass this open rocky space alive."

At that moment, Sergeant John Denny raced back to his wounded comrade, who was "a heavy man," and carried him to safety.

The men who witnessed what one called "a very heroic act" never forgot it. Fifteen years later, Private James Jackson — who fought beside Denny that day — said: "I have often mentioned his bravery to my comrades."

Sergeant Denny was awarded the Congressional Medal of Honor.

In the next few weeks, the Buffalo Soldiers rode almost three thousand miles over trails in the Mimbres and Mogollon mountains that were, they reported, "fearfully rough."

Relentlessly pursued by soldiers, Victorio grew more and more hate-filled and began viciously to mutilate the bodies of the people he killed. Some of his followers feared him so much they left. Still Victorio and the Buffalo Soldiers fought on across the arid landscape like men engaged in some macabre dance of death.

Sergeant George Jordan led twenty-five men on an all-night march to Tularosa, New Mexico, after a settler rode into their camp and said Victorio was attacking the town. The troopers had just finished another grueling day scouting mountain trails when the man arrived.

"My men were in bad condition for a march," said Jordan, "but I explained to them the situation as the rider had put it before me, and that I would leave it to them whether they wanted to continue the march that night or not. They all said that they would go on as far as they could."

The man arrived at the town at daybreak, before the main body of Victorio's warriors had time to get there. When the people realized the men were soldiers, "they came out of their houses waving towels and handkerchiefs for joy."

Jordan directed his men and the settlers in building a stockade and small fort. Victorio attacked at dusk, with his men firing "fully one hundred shots into us before we could gain the shelter of the fort. As the Indians' rifles began to crack, the people rushed to the fort and stockade, all reaching it in safety except our teamsters and two soldiers who were herding the mules and about five hundred head of cattle."

The sergeant directed the rescue of the teamsters and soldiers, as the main body of the company drove the warriors back. Victorio and his men attacked again, and again they were driven back. After exchanging a few more shots, the Apaches retreated toward Mexico.

Victorio was becoming desperate.

Next he turned his warriors toward the western

part of Texas, but several units of the 10th had already been moved there and were waiting for him. Grierson, knowing Victorio could not survive without access to water, had his men guard every water hole and spring near the Mexican border.

Victorio tried in vain to taunt Grierson into clashing with him on the open plain, away from the water holes and springs. At one point the chief even made a scarecrow of the general, clothing it in a dress and bonnet to show his contempt for Grierson's tactics.

But the tactics were working.

Victorio was spotted moving north from near the Mexican border, and three Buffalo Soldiers rode almost one hundred miles in less than a day to deliver the news to Grierson.

In charge of the couriers was Second Lieutenant Henry Ossian Flipper, the first black graduate of the United States Military Academy at West Point. Flipper was the only black officer out of the approximately 2,100 officers in the army.

The young lieutenant was so weary at the end of the/ride that he fell from his horse; he then staggered to his feet and delivered the message to Grierson.

"One of the men unsaddled my horse," Flipper said, "spread the saddle blanket on the ground, I rolled over on it and, with the saddle for a pillow, slept till the sun shining on my face woke me next morning. Then I rode back."

A showdown between the Buffalo Soldiers and Victorio was now inevitable, and it came at a place called Rattlesnake Springs.

Grierson knew Victorio was almost certain to head toward the springs, so he sent two companies racing there. They built small stone "forts" and waited in ambush.

But when the chief came, he sensed that something was wrong and halted. Finally, desperate for water, he moved forward again. The battle for the springs began. Two more companies of Buffalo Soldiers arrived and threw themselves at Victorio in fighting that went on all day.

At twilight, the warriors made one final attempt to reach the springs, but failed. The Buffalo Soldiers chased Victorio for five days, until their horses gave out.

The chief and his people were forced to cross into Mexico again, though they knew Mexican troops were searching for them. The U.S. Government had offered a reward of $3,000 for Victorio's head, and white scalp hunters were also looking for him.

The Apaches wandered aimlessly, no longer able to find refuge. At last they made camp amid three low peaks rising from the desert plain in Chihuahua.

Early one morning Mexican soldiers led by Tar-
ahumara Scouts advanced up the hill. Victorio and
his warriors, the last of their ammunition gone,
fought with their hands.

Then suddenly it was over.

Victorio and seventy-seven of his people lay
dead, while sixty-eight women and children were
captives. Most of the women and children were
sold into slavery in Mexico.

General Pope commended the Buffalo Soldiers
in the Victorio War, saying: "Everything that men
could do they did, and it is little to say that their
services in the field were marked by unusual hardships and difficulties."

The same could have been said about Victorio
and his warriors. Only a few had escaped the
slaughter, and one of them was a partially crippled
and almost blind man in his seventies who was
determined to fight on. His name was Nana.

Nana recruited fifteen warriors, and in the summer of 1881 led them into battle.

They came roaring out of the mountains of Mexico, said General Pope, "like a pack of hungry
wolves, killing everybody they met and stealing
all the horses they could get their hands on."

The Buffalo Soldiers were their first target.

Nana struck at them as they patrolled near the
Texas-New Mexico border, and then battled them
again a few days later.

Sergeant Thomas Shaw, an outstanding marksman, held the most advanced position with a few men. His accurate firing slowed the warrior's charge, and Sergeant George Jordan stopped it completely by "stubbornly holding his ground in an extremely exposed position and gallantly forcing back a much superior number of the enemy and preventing them from surrounding the command."

Shaw was cited for "displaying extraordinary courage under fire," and awarded the Congressional Medal of Honor. Jordan was also awarded the medal for his actions here and at Tularosa many months before. Once again, however, Nana managed to escape.

He next led his warriors south, trying to reach Mexico. Two dozen Buffalo Soldiers and a lieutenant hurried to intercept him. Along the way they were joined by a rancher named George Daly and about twenty cowboys.

At the mouth of Gavilan Canyon near the Mimbres River in southwestern New Mexico, the troopers halted and waited for their comrades to catch up. They had learned enough of Nana's tactics to fear an ambush.

Daly and the cowboys rushed into the deep canyon, however, and the lieutenant followed to protect them.

Nana was waiting.

Shots rang out almost instantly, killing Daly and the officer and wounding several cowboys. The rest, frightened and not knowing what to do, left all the fighting to the handful of troopers.

Sergeant Brent Woods took command.

Woods "promptly called his men, led them in a charge against one side of the cañon, and fought his way desperately to a high piece of ground, driving the Indians before him."

Another sergeant arrived with several men, and the two then led a combined attack that forced Nana to retreat. Woods stayed behind to take care of the wounded, but the other sergeant rushed after the warriors, "carrying his dead and wounded with him."

An officer who arrived after the fighting was over said a miner, "who was with the party of citizens in the action, in speaking to me about it said, 'That Sergt. Woods is a S.O.B. to fight. I had no idea a darky would fight that way. If it had not been for him none of us could have come out of that cañon.' "

Woods was awarded the Congressional Medal of Honor, but of more importance to the Buffalo Soldiers was the fact that Nana had retreated into the mountains of Mexico. They would not have to fight him again.

The men of the 9th had been stationed in New Mexico for six years, following eight hard years headquartered in Texas. Now the army ordered the regiment to Kansas, leaving the men of the 10th to patrol the Southwest.

During the last four years, Geronimo had stayed at San Carlos, trying to farm the desolate soil. But he would not remain much longer.

Heavily armed troops from Fort Apache rode onto the reservation after army authorities killed a medicine man while trying to arrest him. Frightened that the soldiers would attack them next, over seventy men, women, and children fled San Carlos and headed for Mexico. Geronimo helped lead them.

Soon the men of the 10th would follow as Geronimo fought his way into legend as the most feared warrior in the history of the West.

But first they would have to fight an older foe.

It was August, the Moon of Deer Horns Dropping Off.

The Hawk Moon

9

Though the Buffalo Soldiers had fought bravely, made large areas safe for white settlement, and saved the lives of countless people, they received little thanks and no respite from the racism that haunted them.

The safer they made the country for white civilians, the more dangerous white civilians made the country for the soldiers. Some of the worst trouble came from the town adjacent to Fort Concho, Texas, the 10th's headquarters from 1875–82.

The little community of San Angelo, said Grierson, was a "resort for desperate characters and . . . mainly made up of gambling and drinking saloons and other disreputable places."

Both the town and the countryside, said the colonel, were filled with "the greatest set of scoundrels that ever lived on the face of the earth."

Another man described San Angelo's inhabitants as "drunken cowboys, ex-Confederates, pimps and prostitutes."

One night Private William Mace and a few of his friends, all unarmed, were enjoying themselves in a saloon. Suddenly several Texas Rangers came in and attacked them with pistol butts. The soldiers hurried to the fort, grabbed their guns, and headed back to town.

Grierson heard about the incident but didn't realize the soldiers had armed themselves and returned to San Angelo. He demanded an apology from the ranger commander, John Sparks, but instead of apologizing, Sparks insulted him.

By this time the angry soldiers had reached the saloon. Not realizing the rangers were already gone, the soldiers blasted away at the crowd inside. By the time the sound of the last shots died away, one innocent civilian lay dead.

A few months later a crowd of hunters and cowboys surrounded a black soldier in another saloon and cut the sergeant's stripes from his sleeves. He returned to the fort and told several comrades what had happened.

They again armed themselves with carbines and headed to town.

The troopers went straight to the saloon where the sergeant had been humiliated. A vicious gun battle followed, with soldiers and civilians blazing away at each other at close quarters. The civilians finally escaped by shooting out the lights and racing out the back door.

This time, one civilian was killed and two

were wounded. The Buffalo Soldiers also suffered one killed — Private John Brown — and two wounded.

Texas Rangers hurried to Fort Concho to arrest Sergeant George Goldsby for allegedly permitting the soldiers to obtain their guns. But Grierson stopped the rangers, telling them they had no authority on federal property.

Goldsby, the recruit who enlisted from Selma, Alabama, in 1866, deserted rather than allow himself to be tried in a Texas court.

He left behind his part-Cherokee, part-black wife, and a two-year-old son named Crawford. By this time many of the enlisted men were married, and their wives lived on or near the forts. Goldsby would never be heard from again, but his son would go on to become one of the most famous outlaws in the Old West: Cherokee Bill.

A county grand jury indicted Private Mace and nine other Buffalo Soldiers for murder. The sheriff, who was described as a gambler, saloon keeper, and "as great a rascal as any," came with his deputies to arrest them.

Eight of the soldiers deserted before the sheriff arrived. The ninth, Private George Thomas, was shot at the fort and died three days later "from the effects of pistol in the hands of Deputy Sheriff Thomas. . . ."

Mace was caught, tried, and sentenced to death.

He was released, however, when his conviction was overturned on appeal.

None of the rangers or civilians were indicted.

Racial troubles quieted down for a while, and then suddenly erupted with greater violence than ever when two years later, a gambler shot and killed Private Hiram Pinder. Townspeople helped the killer escape and he was never found.

Twelve days later, Private William Watkins was singing and dancing for drinks in the saloon where the rangers had staged their attack several months before.

At about 1 A.M., Watkins quit, saying he was tired. A rancher named Tom McCarthy insisted he continue, and when Watkins refused, McCarthy shot and killed him.

The rancher fled, but was caught by soldiers who turned him over to the sheriff. Instead of jailing McCarthy, however, the sheriff permitted him to remain free.

Afterwards several Buffalo Soldiers, joined by white soldiers from the fort who had also been mistreated in San Angelo, distributed the following circular:

"We, the soldiers of the U.S. Army, do hereby warn the first and last time all citizens and cowboys, etc., of San Angelo and vicinity to recognize our right of way as just and peaceable men. If we do not receive justice and fair play, which we must have, some will suffer — if not the guilty the innocent.

"It has gone too far, justice or death.

"Signed, U.S. Soldiers"

That evening more soldiers went into town and searched for McCarthy, but they didn't find him because the sheriff had hidden the killer in a boardinghouse.

Grierson arrested the men who printed the circular and strengthened the guard to keep troopers on the post.

The civilian authorities finally ordered McCarthy jailed at Ben Ficklin, the county seat, pending action by the grand jury. A company of Buffalo Soldiers rode with the sheriff and his men to make sure they put McCarthy in jail.

Two days later, his brother, who closely resembled him, rode into town. Within minutes, rumors spread among the soldiers at Fort Concho that McCarthy had been released.

Tension rose steadily throughout the day. It culminated at twilight when five white men rode out of the dusk, fired at troopers guarding the fort, then quickly disappeared.

The anger of the Buffalo Soldiers exploded.

Approximately forty troopers grabbed their carbines from the barrack gun racks and stormed into town. A few white soldiers went with them. They grabbed the sheriff and demanded that he hand over McCarthy. The frightened sheriff tried to convince them that McCarthy was still in jail in Ben Ficklin, but the soldiers didn't believe him.

With cowboys and residents scurrying in every direction, the soldiers fired more than 150 shots into a hotel and store. They apparently didn't try to hurt anyone because when the shooting was over, only one man had been slightly wounded. Then the soldiers returned to the fort.

Grierson rushed two companies into San Angelo to guard the civilans, and the state sent twenty-two Texas Rangers. The rangers threatened to storm the post and told Grierson they'd kill any soldier who went into town in the next ten days.

The colonel's reply isn't recorded, but the rangers didn't kill any soldiers or storm the post.

A grand jury met to consider action against the troopers but, remarkably, didn't indict any. McCarthy was indicted for first-degree murder and taken to Austin for a quick trial before an all-white jury.

According to one newspaper reporter, the jurors were out just long enough to write their verdict: "Not Guilty!"

Grierson was required to write a report on the disturbance for General Edward O. Ord, commander of the Department of Texas.

Ord had once written Colonel Shafter describing black soldiers as "ruffians" and urging that the black regiments be broken up (an action Shafter supported). Ord had also requested that all black soldiers under his command be replaced by white soldiers.

Grierson described the racial provocations the black troopers had endured through the years and listed all the men who had been murdered with impunity by white civilians.

Ord was unimpressed by the racial discrimination aimed at the Buffalo Soldiers, but was transferred before he could give an official response. General C. C. Auger, who replaced Ord, was equally unimpressed and warned Grierson the regiment would be disbanded if there was another disturbance.

Although the threat was made at almost the same time Brent Woods, George Jordan, Thomas Shaw, and other Buffalo Soldiers were risking their lives to protect white settlers, the soldiers knew there was much support for Auger's racial position among civilians, politicians, and many top military men.

Grierson wrote to a friend, complaining about "the prejudice and unjust discrimination that I have had to meet and for nearly fifteen years contend against."

The men were well aware that many officers and politicians wanted to make the army all white.

Legislation had been introduced in Congress in

Henry O. Flipper, the first black man to graduate from West Point.

A long march of Indian prisoners captured by Lieutenant Colonel Custer.

Buffalo Soldiers of the 10th Cavalry at Fort Custer, Montana, in 1880.

*Water tanks carried by mules for the Buffalo Soldiers,
Fort Verde, Arizona, 1887.*

Ulysses S. Grant, President of the United States from 1869–1877.

*George Buell,
who was a
Lieutenant Colonel
when he commanded
the Buffalo Soldiers.*

The 10th Cavalry hospital, fortified with hay.

Geronimo, the great Apache leader.

Sitting Bull, famous Sioux chief.

Battle with Lieutenant Colonel Custer as depicted by an unidentified American Indian artist.

Lieutenant Colonel George Custer.

"The Ghost Dancers" painted by Mary Irvin Wright.

Men in the 10th Cavalry troop, probably at Fort Apache in Arizona.

Monument to the Buffalo Soldiers unveiled at Fort Leavenworth, Kansas; July 26, 1992.

1876 and 1878 to eliminate the black regiments. General Sherman testified in support, saying: "If I were compelled to choose 5,000 men to go into a fight with, I would rather take 5,000 white men."

In his annual report for 1880, General J. M. Schofield of the United States Military Academy denounced the appointment of black youths as cadets.

"As well might the common farm horse be entered in a four-mile race against the best blood inherited from a long line of English racers," said the West Point superintendent.

Army officials had even introduced segregation into the schools run by chaplains on many bases. If there were both black and white soldiers, the army required separate schools for the two races or separate classrooms if there was just one school.

Sometimes segregation was carried to extremes that were almost laughable. Separate rooms were built for the post guards at Camp Supply, so that white privates and corporals wouldn't find themselves under the command of a black sergeant.

Before the separate rooms were built, complained the wife of one white officer, there was "a daily mingling of white and colored troops which often brings a colored sergeant over a white corporal and privates."

The racial prejudice directed at the soldiers by civilians came from every segment of Texas society, including the most influential.

No matter where they turned and no matter how well they fought, the Buffalo Soldiers collided with the solid wall of racism. Though many black men had fought and died in Union Army artillery regiments during the Civil War — including the battles of Vicksburg, Fort Donelson, Fort Pillow, and Milliken's Bend — military officials and Congress continued to restrict them to infantry and cavalry regiments in the post-Civil War army.

"It is wrong, and Congress should place these brave black soldiers upon the same footing as the white troops," wrote ex-Sergeant Major Williams.

Lieutenant Richard Pratt of the 10th protested that he failed to see how having racially segregated regiments "would accord with the [14th Constitutional] amendment that there must be no distinction."

But racial difficulties for the soldiers were increasing rather than decreasing, and the men of the 10th were glad when their headquarters was moved to Fort Davis (named after Jefferson Davis when the post was established in 1854. Davis, who was then U.S. secretary of war, would go on to become president of the Confederacy during the Civil War).

Davis was a remote post in southwest Texas not far from the border with Mexico, and its isolation from white settlers was a welcome respite for the soldiers.

The fort had been destroyed during the Civil

War, and the Buffalo Soldiers rebuilt it, mostly of stone and adobe bricks. In addition to barracks and officers' quarters, it contained a hospital, 1,200-volume library, chapel, and school.

Each of the four black regiments was stationed there at one time or another, beginning in 1867 when four companies of the 9th rode in.

Besides working on the buildings, the soldiers used picks and shovels to carve out roads through the twisting canyons that led to the fort.

The first Buffalo Soldiers to serve at Davis clashed frequently with raiding warriors, especially Apaches. After one battle, several troopers were returning with captured clothing and supplies when they spotted some friends at work in a quarry.

The men stopped and dressed themselves in the Apache clothing. Then, led by Sergeant George Washington, the yelling and screaming soldiers raced toward the quarry.

"You can imagine how fast those men ran trying to get back to the post," Washington wrote a friend.

By the time the 10th was transferred to Davis, the area was largely quiet. Most of the fighting had shifted westward, and the soldiers were "engaged in working on roads, constructing telegraph lines, building store rooms and stables at post. Also escort duty."

It was much more peaceful for most of the men

than at Fort Concho, but there was major trouble brewing for Lieutenant Flipper.

He was well received by some of the officers in the regiment, especially the younger ones, but his presence was bitterly resented by others. They were especially incensed because one of the few white women in the area often went riding with him.

Flipper found the racial atmosphere at Davis fairly relaxed, however, for he had endured four years of isolation at West Point. During all that time, no other cadets had even spoken to him except on official duty or when none of their friends was watching.

"There was no society for me to enjoy," Flipper recalled of his lonely years at the academy. "No friends, male or female, for me to visit, or with whom I could have any social intercourse, so absolute was my isolation."

When his company was transferred to Fort Davis, Flipper was placed in charge of the post commissary. As commissary officer he was responsible for buying all supplies for both troops and animals. The twenty-five-year-old carried out his duties with unusual efficiency and dedication.

Once, gravely ill with malaria, he ordered two troopers to carry him on a stretcher to his office. There he somehow managed to pay all the post's suppliers and civilian employees, before having to be carried back to his quarters on the stretcher.

Flipper's military career progressed well until the post commander, who was very friendly to him, was replaced by Colonel Shafter (Grierson was still at Fort Concho).

Within weeks, Shafter arrested Flipper on charges of embezzling $3,791.77. Officers accused of nonviolent crimes were normally confined to their quarters, but Shafter had Flipper arrested at gunpoint and locked in a small windowless cell in the guardhouse.

The commander even barred several visitors who had come to see Flipper, calling one man a "drunken nigger that had been a servant in the garrison."

Grierson vigorously defended Flipper, who charged he was the victim of a plot by Shafter and two other officers. Flipper was confined for several months, then acquitted of the embezzlement charges.

The court-martial found him guilty of "conduct unbecoming an officer," however, and on June 30, 1882, he was banished from the service. The sentence was incredibly harsh.

A white officer convicted of embezzling over $23,000 several years before had been sentenced to a reprimand and suspension from his command for four months. Another white officer convicted of fraud and conspiracy in the handling of gov-

ernment money, was suspended from his rank for
twelve years and allowed to collect half-pay all
that time.

Neither of the white officers was found guilty
of "conduct unbecoming an officer."

Captain Merritt Barber of the 16th Infantry
Regiment, who voluntarily defended Flipper during his court-martial, said of the verdict: "The
department commander, the secretary of war, and
the president of the United States [Chester A.
Arthur], in dismissing the army's only black officer, tacitly voiced their opinion that no Negro was
fit to bear the responsibility and prestige attached
to the uniform of an officer of the United States
Army."

The Buffalo Soldiers and black Americans were
stunned and angered by Flipper's dismissal, but
many of the officers in the 10th approved.

Major Anson Mills was a native of Texas who
had once canceled a party several lieutenants
planned in honor of Flipper.

"I do not think that he was treated exactly
right," Mills said, "but I would not for a moment
advocate his reinstatement. . . . His commission
made him an officer and gentleman, but then, you
know, one couldn't meet a colored man on social
equality."

Another officer said the verdict would have
been unfair if Flipper had been white, but that a

black man shouldn't have been made an officer in the first place.

"Our wives and daughters must be considered," he declared, apparently believing that commissioning black officers should depend on whether or not there were white women on the post.

The 10th Cavalry did not have another black officer for almost twenty years.

Flipper remained in the West, becoming a highly respected mining engineer, and life at Fort Davis returned to normal. The post began to attract all kinds of people, and they seemed to get along well.

"Fort Davis became a regular melting pot," said one civilian. "Foreigners [European immigrants in the army] married Mexican women; Negroes married Mexican women. Mexicans do not draw the color line. I knew one Mexican woman who married a white man . . . while her aunt was married to a very black Negro. An Irish girl married a Jew, and her brother a Mexican girl. Fort Davis had a regular crazy quilt population."

More and more settlers_____hers began to drift into the area w_____re now just a memo_____Ari_____

and ranc_____

where Apache raids we_____

en southern New Mexico and

d been the scene of several

Geronimo and his followers

1, were now quiet.

Apaches returned to San

Carlos in 1883, after General George Crook promised them fair treatment from the government. Geronimo and Chato came back from the mountains of Mexico in early 1884 and began competing with each other to see who could develop the best farm at San Carlos.

Crook, who made sure the agent delivered all the promised supplies, was able to say proudly that "not an outrage or depredation of any kind" was committed by the Apaches for more than a year.

But Crook was increasingly unpopular among the whites for his fair treatment of the Apaches, and they bitterly attacked both him and Geronimo. The newspapers invented atrocity stories about Geronimo and urged vigilantes to hang him.

"When a man tried to do right," Geronimo said, "such stories ought not to be put in the newspapers."

In the spring of 1885, Geronimo fled from the reservation again after hearing rumors he was going to be arrested and hanged.

The men of the 10th rode directly into the ble that was upt, for they ha
been Terri

about to transferred to Arizona They left Fort Davis in early and was two-mile column of men It marked the fi regimental band. th regiment's nineteen-year history companies had been together, but quickly split up again.

Most of the men were scattered among Forts Apache, Verde, Thomas, and Grant, while Grierson and one company were assigned to headquarters at Whipple Barracks.

The day Grierson reported to General Crook was the day Geronimo, Nana, Nachez, Chihuahua, and Mangas fled San Carlos. Almost 150 followers went with them, including 38 warriors, 8 boys "old enough to fight," and 100 women and children.

When Geronimo broke out, the newspapers had a field day.

"GERONIMO'S BAND OF THUGS," read a headline in *The New York Times*. An editorial in the same issue called Geronimo and his people "wretches who are worse than wild beasts. . . . We do not see why those who may survive should not be hanged."

Crook threw every available man into the field.

Five companies of Buffalo Soldiers rode out of Fort Grant, heading toward the Chiricahua Mountains near the border with Mexico. Over one hundred other Buffalo Soldiers rode out of Fort Bayard in southwestern New Mexico, scouting along rugged trails in the Black and Mogollon mountains.

While those men were still out, Geronimo and his warriors were spotted moving toward Mexico. More Buffalo Soldiers were sent in pursuit "through southern part of Arizona and New Mexico and part of northern Mexico . . . when pursuit was abandoned and [the troops] returned to the station; during the march the men and horses suffered from hunger and fatigue to an uncomfortable degree."

The Buffalo Soldiers rode hundreds of miles in a vain and weary search for Geronimo.

In the spring of 1886, however, Geronimo and his followers were spotted by the Buffalo Soldiers in southern Arizona. The soldiers chased the Apaches more than fifty miles, forcing them back into Mexico.

But Geronimo could find no rest there, either. While American soldiers, guided by Apache scouts, hunted him from the north, Mexican soldiers accompanied by scouts pursued him through the canyons and across the mountains of the Sierra Madre.

American scalp hunters were also on the trail of the fleeing men, women, and children. The Mexicans paid $100 for a scalp belonging to an Apache man, $50 for a woman's, and $25 for the scalp of a child. The warriors and their families were well aware that if the white scalp hunters or Mexicans found them, they would be given no chance to surrender.

Geronimo's hiding place in Mexico was finally discovered by Chato, who was now a sergeant of scouts in the army, and by Alchise, Cochise's youngest son. They persuaded the hard-pressed leader to talk to Crook.

Geronimo chose the meeting place, a canyon several miles south of the Arizona border called Cañon de los Embudos (Canyon of the Tricksters).

The talks lasted three days. In the end, Geronimo agreed to surrender, along with Nachez, Chihuahua, and all their followers.

The night after the agreement was reached, a white man came to the Apaches' camp and sold them whiskey. While Geronimo and several of the others drank, the peddler told them they would be murdered by whites once they crossed into Arizona.

"I feared treachery," Geronimo declared.

Once again he fled toward the mountains of Mexico. This time less than fifty people, including Nachez, went with him. Most of the people were related to Geronimo and Nachez, so the group was composed largely of two families who were about to be pursued by several thousand soldiers.

Sheridan ordered that all the men, women, and children who had surrendered be shipped to prison in Saint Augustine, Florida. Sheridan said they would be imprisoned for however long the government felt like holding them.

Crook resigned in disgust at this treatment of the Apaches and asked for a transfer to another command. It was quickly granted.

The task of subduing Geronimo was then given to General Nelson A. Miles, who thought all Apaches were ignorant and brutal.

"With our superior intelligence and modern appliances, we should be able to surpass all the advantages possessed by the savages," Miles declared.

Five thousand soldiers were placed under his command — approximately one fifth of the army — to try and defeat Geronimo, the eighteen warriors who were still with him, and a smaller group led by Chief Mangas.

Miles also hired Apache scouts to act as trackers.

Soldiers were assigned to guard every pass and water hole along the Mexican border, but Geronimo managed to elude them and cross into Arizona. There he and his warriors swept through the Santa Cruz Valley, killing several cowboys. Then they struck at a ranch just north of Nogales and killed a man, woman, and child.

Buffalo Soldiers were the first to arrive on the scene. Under the guidance of Lieutenant Thomas C. Lebo, they wrapped the bodies in blankets and buried them, and then took off in pursuit of Geronimo.

His trail led south into Mexico, and for almost a week the troopers followed "the hostiles rapidly for over two hundred miles" through canyons and over craggy peaks. They slowly gained ground on the Apaches, whose weary horses had been driven almost as far as they could go.

Geronimo turned to fight at the top of a steep slope in the Pinito Mountains of Sonora, knowing the soldiers would pay a heavy price if they tried to charge him.

The soldiers charged up "rugged cliffs almost inaccessible."

They were met with a massive burst of rifle fire that killed Private Joseph Follis and wounded Corporal Edward Scott, while the rest of the men sought cover behind boulders.

Scott was left lying in the open "with a serious wound, exposed to the enemy's fire." Lieutenant Powhattan Clarke raced across the open ground as the Apaches "fairly plowed up the ground with bullets," said one Buffalo Soldier, "and never took no notice what was going on no more than if the man had just fell down in a field somewhere."

Clarke was awarded the Congressional Medal of Honor, and General Miles said that all of the officers and men "evinced great bravery."

Geronimo and his men finally retreated, leaving behind two dead and one wounded.

The next several weeks brought more raids, and Miles's five thousand men seemed powerless to stop them. The country was simply too harsh, and both men and horses were breaking down.

"It is a country rough beyond description,"

wrote one of the officers, "covered everywhere with cactus and full of rattlesnakes and other undesirable companions of that sort."

Miles sought help from Kayitah and Martine, two ex-followers of Geronimo who were now living peacefully at San Carlos. He promised them a reward if they could find him.

The two tracked Geronimo and Nachez to a canyon.

Miles made excuse after excuse not to meet with Geronimo and even suggested that other officers catch Geronimo off guard and murder him. But finally the two met.

Miles promised Geronimo and the others a large reservation in Florida "with horses and wagons" and promised "no one will harm you."

"I will quit the warpath and live at peace hereafter," Geronimo replied.

Geronimo and his followers were taken to Fort Bowie, then placed on a train to Florida. Kayitah and Martine were among those shipped off to prison.

While all of this was going on, Chato and several other Apache leaders were in Washington at the invitation of President Grover Cleveland. Chato said he was anxious to return home to his farm at San Carlos, but took time to plead for help in rescuing his wife and two children, who were being held in slavery in Mexico.

Officials presented him with a silver peace

medal and said they would consider his request for help. Within days, however, he and the others were on their way to prison in Florida by order of the president at General Sherman's urging.

All of the Apaches living peacefully at San Carlos were forced onto trains the day Geronimo surrendered, to be taken to prison in Florida.

Even the scouts who worked for the army were treated as prisoners of war, and some were arrested while still wearing their army uniforms.

The Buffalo Soldiers were assigned the unpleasant task of rounding up the more than four hundred men, women, and children at San Carlos.

The soldiers formed the Apaches into a column that was two miles long, then marched them ninety miles to the railroad depot at Holbrook, Arizona.

In addition to men, women, and children, there were 1,600 horses and 3,000 dogs. A few Apache scouts who hadn't been arrested led the column "with their carbines always ready for instant action."

The Buffalo Soldiers kept close watch on a band of cowboys who followed the column, waiting for a chance to murder any man, woman, or child they could get their hands on.

The Buffalo Soldiers gave them no such opportunities, however.

The last night before the train pulled out, a soldier standing guard looked toward the Apache camp in a dry river bottom. The sight that greeted his eyes, he declared in awe, was "a spectacle that perhaps no man will see again."

Spread out below him were hundreds of fires glowing like stars in the darkness, "and around each fire was a group of Indians, dancing and singing in celebration of their coming journey to see the 'Great Father' in Washington. Drums were sounding incessantly, and the frenzied, monotonous chant of the Indians pervading the night air, and the mournful howling of the thousands of dogs over all (they seemed to scent a catastrophe), made a curious and lasting impression, never to be forgotten."

The next morning the Apaches were loaded onto eighteen railroad cars. The heat was stifling, but all the windows had been nailed shut to prevent escapes.

When the train finally pulled out of the station, "the thousands of deserted dogs tried frantically to keep abreast of the moving cars, every one howling with all his might."

Gradually the dogs fell behind and finally could run no more. That day and for several days afterwards the cowboys had "great sport" shooting them. All the Apaches' horses were rounded up and sold at bargain prices to settlers.

The Buffalo Soldiers rode back to Fort Apache, camping overnight along the way. But now there were no fires glowing in the darkness, except the ones they made.

The only leader still out now was Mangas. The army offered a reward of $1,500 for him, dead or alive, and a few weeks later he surrendered to a detachment of Buffalo Soldiers out searching for him.

With him was his wife Huera, who was Victorio's daughter; two other women; five children; and two warriors. One of the warriors was an old man.

All the others had been captured in Mexico several days before, and murdered by Apache-hating Tarahumaras for the scalp money.

The Buffalo Soldiers began collecting the supplies carried by Mangas's people. One of the women pleaded with them to be allowed to keep the bag of cornmeal she had been carrying, and they gave it back to her.

The Apache Wars were over, and they ended even before Mangas was captured.

Geronimo's surrender in Skeleton Canyon in the fall of 1886 marked the end of the Apache struggle for freedom that had begun against the Spanish almost three hundred years before. His surrender, for all practical purposes, also marked the end of the Indian Wars in the United States.

Looking back, it was surprising it had taken the government so long to defeat a people who were so vastly outnumbered. There were only 20,000 Comanches when they were at their strongest and fewer than 2,000 Kiowas at a time when 90,000 settlers crossed their lands in a single year.

The Apaches never numbered more than a few hundred.

Now virtually all Native Americans had been confined to reservations or prisons, though some would still fight back in the years ahead.

But though defeat had already come, there would be one final, desperate attempt to bring back the old way of life on the Great Plains. It would happen on a barren reservation in South Dakota, with a lonely, windswept creek running through it called Chankpe Opi Wakpala: Wounded Knee.

The Buffalo Soldiers would be there.

They would ride onto the Great Sioux Reservation in November, the Hawk Moon.

The Time of the Buffalo Soldiers

10

So much had changed since the Buffalo Soldiers first came west, both for them and for the people they fought.

In a little over two decades, the Comanches, Kiowas, Arapahos, Apaches, Lakotas, Cheyennes, Nez Percés, and other nations had been driven from their lands throughout the Great Plains, after fighting for generations to keep them.

With the surrender of Geronimo and the capture of Mangas, all of the great Native American leaders were now dead, in prison, or confined to reservations.

Crazy Horse had been one of the last to surrender. He brought his starving people into Fort Robinson, Nebraska, in the spring of 1877, in exchange for General Miles's promise of a reservation in the Powder River country of what is now Wyoming.

The great war leader and his people came defiantly, almost one thousand strong, singing battle songs and waving their weapons before they gave them up. Pawnee, Crow, Shoshone, Arapaho, and Lakota scouts and policemen hired by the army rode beside them to make sure they surrendered.

Soldiers took the more than two thousand horses that Crazy Horse's people brought with them, and now the Lakotas could neither flee nor fight. Then, instead of giving them a reservation, Miles issued orders for Crazy Horse to be imprisoned on the Dry Tortugas islands off the coast of Florida. When he resisted arrest by a soldier and by a Lakota policeman who had once been his friend, Crazy Horse was killed.

Ironically, during the years the Buffalo Soldiers were hunting and killing Native Americans in the West, black Americans were being hunted and killed in the South. Blacks who voted or who managed to buy their own farms, "secure pleasant homes," and become financially independent were the special targets of violence.

And so, while Native Americans were being driven onto reservations in the West, black Americans in the South were being driven back to the plantations many had left when slavery ended. Both groups were increasingly forced to the edges of society, stripped of power, and subjected to white control.

When Custer was defeated at the Battle of the Little Big Horn in 1876, whites used the defeat as an argument for removal of federal troops from the

South, where they'd been stationed to protect black people.

In July, the same month the nation's newspapers filled column after column with news of Custer's defeat, they also printed column after column about a massacre in Hamburg, South Carolina. There, following a Fourth of July picnic, an ex-Confederate general led a mob that murdered several black men. Soon afterwards, the mob leader — Matthew C. Butler — was elected to the U.S. Senate.

The lives of Native Americans and black Americans alike were of little value to the majority of white Americans. No one was convicted for the murder of the black men in Hamburg or for the murders of thousands of other black people throughout the South, but angry whites cried out for revenge for Custer's death.

At approximately the same time the army was relentlessly hunting Lakotas in the months after Custer's death, ex-Sergeant Major Williams wrote that "the spirit of violence and persecution" against black people in the South was raging "with renewed fury."

In 1878, after the widespread slaughter of blacks who tried to vote in the South, one man said they had as much chance to survive there as "a cat in hell without claws."

Black Southerners pleaded with U.S. Government officials for protection, but the officials refused to help. Thousands of desperate blacks then fled to the West seeking some place where they could live their lives in peace and freedom.

They staked out homesteads on the prairie; settled in Leavenworth, Dodge City, Abilene, and other communities; and built almost thirty all-black towns in Kansas and Indian Territory.

In 1885, when the men of the 9th were transferred to Wyoming, Nebraska, and Utah, they found black civilians working the land and laboring in the towns alongside whites.

The almost three hundred Buffalo Soldiers who were transferred to Fort Robinson in the Pine Ridge country of northwestern Nebraska found many black civilians in the nearby town of Crawford. It was a welcome discovery for the men, for visits to the town provided a welcome relief from what had become a life of boredom.

Several of the original Buffalo Soldiers were still in the army, including Stance and Jordan. But now there were also many younger men, such as Edward Lee Baker, Jr., who was born in a California-bound wagon train on the North Platte River, Wyoming, in 1865.

Another new trooper was Horace W. Bivins, Jr., the son of a farmer who built the first church and school for free black people on Virginia's eastern shore. Whites burned the school to the ground within hours after it was completed, but Bivins's father rebuilt it within a week.

Unlike most of the original Buffalo Soldiers, Bivins was well educated. He had attended Wayland Seminary in Washington, D.C., and Hampton Institute in Virginia (in 1879, the government began sending many young Lakotas, Kiowas, Cheyennes, Arapahos, and other Native Americans to Hampton, a black school, to "civilize" them).

The fact that a man like Bivins would choose to join the army indicated how few opportunities there still were for black people in late nineteenth-century America.

There was little for the men at Fort Robinson to do except patrol the Pine Ridge Reservation in South Dakota, a few miles to the north.

Another two hundred Buffalo Soldiers were assigned to Fort Niobrara, Nebraska, almost 170 miles east of Fort Robinson, and they were also delighted to find many black civilians in the adjacent town of Valentine.

The soldiers at Niobrara often patrolled the Rosebud Reservation in South Dakota, which was adjacent to Pine Ridge.

Red Cloud, the chief whose warriors had once driven the army from all its forts in the Powder River country, lived quietly at Pine Ridge.

Sitting Bull, still defiantly resisting white efforts

to take the Lakotas' remaining lands, lived further north on the Standing Rock Reservation, which straddled the border between North and South Dakota.

The Buffalo Soldiers, like the Lakota warriors, often relieved the boredom by talking about past battles. But once in a while, the peace was suddenly shattered.

In 1886, a gang of outlaws robbed the stagecoach carrying the payroll to Fort Robinson.

Sergeant Emanuel Stance, who'd been the first Buffalo Soldier to win the Medal of Honor, led a detachment that chased the thieves more than twenty miles. The troopers eventually lost the trail, however, and returned to the fort.

The next year, the sergeant, who had survived twenty-nine years of battles and harsh weather, was found murdered a few miles from the fort. One private said Stance had a reputation for being "dirty mean" to his men, and an officer said he was probably killed by "the men of his own troop."

All duty was suspended the day of his funeral "as a matter of respect" to the man who'd joined up that autumn day in 1866. Sergeant Major Jeremiah Jones led the men in marching formation to the post hospital, where they placed Stance's body on a wagon.

Then they marched to the post cemetery, followed by the carriages of the officers' families. Sixteen men fired a salute as Stance's body was lowered into the ground. His murderer was never found.

The months following Stance's death were quiet ones at Fort Robinson, but conditions were growing steadily worse just to the north on the Pine Ridge Reservation. On ration days, which came about once every two weeks, hundreds of women lined up for hours to receive the food doled out by the agent.

The amount given grew smaller and smaller, and soon it was barely enough for the people to live on.

By the beginning of the winter of 1889, the Lakotas were largely destitute and hungry. In early 1890, President Benjamin Harrison stunned them by throwing open millions of acres of their land to white settlers.

"They made us many promises," said one old man about U.S. Government officials, "more than I can remember, but they never kept but one; they promised to take our land and they took it."

Congress also ordered drastic cuts in the food allotments. Thousands of cattle were roaming the reservation, but the government agent refused to allow any to be killed for food.

While all this was happening, the Buffalo Soldiers at Forts Robinson and Niobrara continued to perform "ordinary garrison duty," such as keeping the roads open in winter and escorting wagon trains carrying supplies for the forts.

Far to the south, however, some of their comrades in the 10th were having a much more exciting time.

On May 11, 1889, troopers James Wheeler and Thornton Hams, along with Major Joseph W. Wham and nine black soldiers from the 24th Infantry Regiment, were escorting an army payroll to Fort Grant, Arizona.

Suddenly, reported Wham, "a large boulder, weighing several tons . . . rolled into the road and stopped."

It was not unusual for boulders to block the roads, so Wheeler, Hams, and the other soldiers immediately went "down the gorge to the front to clear the way. They were nearly all at the boulder when a signal shot was fired from the ledge of rocks about fifty feet to the right, which was instantly followed by a volley . . . of fifteen or twenty shots."

The bullets poured down on the men, said Wham, "from six well constructed stone forts."

The soldiers fought back "from such poor cover, as could be instantly found. The Sergeant [Benjamin Brown] made his entire fight from open ground. However, the position which I occupied with the main party was but little better, being enfiladed by both the robber flanks."

"The brigands" fired hundreds of shots, and within seconds almost every soldier had been wounded at least once and some twice.

Wheeler and Hams were wounded "while

bravely doing their duty under a murderous cross-fire."

Private Hamilton Lewis, driver of the pay wagon, was "shot through the stomach, but the noble fellow was undaunted, and while blood gushed from his terrible wound, he heroically continued to fight. . . ."

Sergeant Brown, "though shot through the abdomen, did not quit the field until again wounded, this time through the arm."

Corporal Isaiah Mays somehow escaped the gunfire and "walked and crawled two miles to Cottonwood ranch and gave the alarm. . . ."

By the time he returned, the robbers had fled with the $29,000 payroll.

Wham said their leader was, "as is now almost certainly shown by [U.S.] Marshal Meade, Gilbert Webb, a reputed ex-member of the 'Mormon Legion,' 'Destroying Angels,' and participant in the 'Mountain Meadow Massacre.' "

Webb and several other men underwent one of the longest trials on record in the Southwest, but all were found not guilty. None of the money was ever recovered, and the "Wham Paymaster Robbery" remains one of the most puzzling crimes in the history of the West.

Wham praised the conduct of the soldiers involved, saying: "I was a soldier in Grant's old regiment during the entire [Civil] war. It was justly proud of its record of sixteen battles and of the reflected glory of its old Colonel, the 'Great Commander.' But I never witnessed better courage or better fighting than shown by these colored soldiers on May 11, 1889. . . ."

Sergeant Brown and Corporal Mays were awarded the Congressional Medal of Honor for their valor, while Wheeler, Hams, and five others were awarded Certificates of Merit.

Hundreds of miles to the north, the quiet routine of the Buffalo Soldiers of the 9th was also about to end.

In November 1890, black cavalrymen were suddenly ordered to the Pine Ridge and Rosebud reservations.

The soldiers were sent because the Lakotas, pushed to the edge of despair, had embraced a religion that promised to bring back their vanished way of life. The religion was called the Ghost Dance, and it was started by a thirty-four-year-old Paiute shaman named Wovoka. His followers believed that he was the messiah.

Native Americans from throughout the Great Plains journeyed to his home in Nevada, including the Lakota chiefs, Good Thunder and Short Bull.

When they returned, Good Thunder began preaching the new religion at Pine Ridge, and Short Bull did the same at Rosebud.

"The earth is getting old, and I will make it new for my chosen people, the Indians, who are to inhabit it, and among them will be all those of their ancestors who have died," Wovoka said.

He promised to cover the earth with new soil, which would bury all the white people, and allow the earth to "be covered with sweet-grass and running water and trees, and herds of buffalo and ponies will stray over it, that my red children may eat and drink, hunt and rejoice."

In order for all of this to happen, Wovoka declared, the people must learn the Ghost Dance. The dance was basically a round dance where men and women formed a circle and joined hands, then sidestepped to the left.

It also incorporated elements from the Sun Dance, which the Indian Bureau had banned a few years earlier in its attempts to wipe out all Native American religious beliefs.

"You must not hurt anybody or do harm to anyone," Wovoka taught. "You must not fight. Do right always."

Whites were terrified of the dancers, however.

"We had begged for life," said Red Cloud, "and the white men thought we wanted theirs."

More and more Lakotas joined the Ghost Dancers, searching desperately for hope in the midst of the darkest times they had ever known.

White squatters on the Pine Ridge Reservation demanded military protection.

"Indians are dancing in the snow and are wild

and crazy," the agent at Pine Ridge telegraphed to Washington. "We need protection and we need it now."

And so the first troops were sent, but there was little for them to do. The men of the 9th set up camp next to a village filled with children playing and women quietly going about their chores.

A former agent at Pine Ridge advised authorities to "let the dance continue. The coming of the troops has frightened the Indians. . . . If the troops remain, trouble is sure to come."

A list of "fomenters of disturbances" among the Ghost Dancers was telegraphed to the Indian Bureau in Washington, which forwarded it to General Miles's headquarters in Chicago.

Sitting Bull's name was on it. Sitting Bull had never ceased fighting for his people's rights and insisted that they hold onto as many of their traditional ways as possible.

"It is not necessary that eagles should be crows," he declared in resisting white attempts to wipe out Lakota culture.

Miles assumed that arresting the aging chief would end the dances and the threat many whites felt from the new religious beliefs.

At dawn on December 15, Indian policemen surrounded Sitting Bull's cabin on the Standing Rock Reservation. White cavalrymen waited out of sight in case they were needed.

Sitting Bull was informed by Lieutenant Bull

Head, the policeman in charge, that he was under arrest.

"You think you are going to take him," shouted Catch-the-Bear, one of the leading Ghost Dancers. "You shall not do it!"

Catch-the-Bear fired at and wounded Bull Head, who shot wildly and hit Sitting Bull. At virtually the same instant, Sergeant Red Tomahawk shot Sitting Bull through the back of the head, killing him instantly.

While men died all around him, Sitting Bull's circus horse — a gift from Buffalo Bill — raised his hoof to shake hands as he had been trained to do at the sound of gunfire.

The fighting took the lives of eight of Sitting Bull's followers and six policemen. The chief's seventeen-year-old son, Crowfoot, was one of the dead.

Panic-stricken and afraid the soldiers would kill them next, hundreds of Sitting Bull's followers fled the reservation.

Some sought refuge in the camps of the Ghost Dancers deep in the Badlands, while others raced to Red Cloud's camp at Pine Ridge.

Several dozen joined Chief Big Foot at the Cheyenne River Reservation near the center of the state, but a white squatter from Pine Ridge told them the army was going to arrest all the men "and then move you to an island in the ocean in the east."

The squatter urged them to go to Pine Ridge "right away if you want to save your lives. If you don't listen to me, you will get in trouble."

And so Big Foot led his people toward the reservation and what he thought was safety.

The Buffalo Soldiers were still camped peacefully near "an Indian village with dogs barking and the sound of children's voices and the hum of squaws as they busied themselves with . . . housekeeping. . . ."

The peacefulness would not last much longer.

Members of the 7th Cavalry made their camp in the valley of Wounded Knee Creek, about twenty miles north of the Pine Ridge Agency. The agency consisted of a hotel, boarding school, churches, government warehouses, and several homes. Almost six thousand Lakotas had been driven into the agency or had come on their own since Sitting Bull was killed.

Miles sent soldiers scurrying after Big Foot and the hundreds of people with him, not knowing the chief was voluntarily coming into the agency. His group was moving slowly because Big Foot had developed pneumonia, but the soldiers had trouble finding them.

Alarmed that the group might be trying to join the Ghost Dancers in the Badlands, Miles ordered a detachment of Buffalo Soldiers to join the search.

The soldiers rode far to the northwest of the agency, but could find no trace of the chief or his people. The weather was bitterly cold.

"You late [laid] out in the cold like a dog," said Private Charles Creek, "[often] not in a tent because the Indians gonna sneak up on you."

Cavalrymen from the 7th finally found Big Foot and his followers near a place called Porcupine Butte. Both sides formed a battle line.

Big Foot, barely able to walk, carried a white flag and went out to meet the soldiers. The major in charge ordered him to take his people to a camp on Wounded Knee Creek, and the chief readily agreed.

They reached the camp at twilight.

The creek was small and lined with brush and cottonwoods, as it meandered through a valley only a half-mile wide. Officers ordered that the people be counted: there were 120 men and 230 women and children.

That night more soldiers arrived and set up four rapid-firing Hotchkiss guns on a hill overlooking the camp.

"There was a great uneasiness among the Indians all night," remembered one warrior who was there. They "were fearful that they were to be killed."

The next day many Lakotas, along with white settlers and reporters, came out to watch the arrest of Big Foot. Though the chief didn't know it, the army had ordered that he and his people be sent to a military prison in Omaha.

Many of the spectators sat in horse-drawn buggies, as if they were going to a picnic. Big Foot, who had grown worse during the night, half-sat and half-lay outside a tent.

A reporter said he saw a group of "eight or ten Indian boys dressed in the grey school uniforms of that period. The fun they were having as they played . . . carried the mind for a fleeting moment back to the days of boyhood."

A detachment of Buffalo Soldiers had patrolled Wounded Knee Creek the day before, but were now back at the agency.

Colonel James Forsyth ordered all the Lakotas to surrender their weapons. A man named Black Coyote refused, saying he had paid good money for his rifle. A struggle followed, and the rifle accidentally discharged.

Warriors and soldiers immediately began to shoot, stab, and club each other to death.

A reporter said that as soon as the first shot was fired, he saw "the spectators, some in their buggies and others clambering in pell-mell, whipping their teams into a stampede . . . (as) stray bullets were whizzing among them."

Big Foot tried to raise himself up to see what was happening and was immediately killed by a volley of shots.

Soldiers began ripping the area with the Hotchkiss guns, each gun firing a two-pound shell almost every second. Men, women, and children were cut down in a mass of screaming humanity.

Some of the Lakotas managed to flee as far as three miles before the soldiers killed them.

The fighting lasted less than an hour. By the time it was over, up to three hundred Lakota men, women, and children were dead or dying. The exact number has never been determined.

Twenty-five of the 7th Cavalry soldiers were killed and thirty-nine wounded, many by their comrades' bullets.

The roar of the Hotchkiss guns was heard at the agency, and angry warriors rushed out to strike the cavalrymen wherever they could find them. The commander of the 7th sent an urgent message asking the Buffalo Soldiers for reinforcements.

The soldiers had just finished a fifty-mile scout and were far from the agency when an exhausted messenger brought word "of the fight of the 7th Cavalry with Big Foot's band."

It was almost 10 P.M. when the Buffalo Soldiers saddled up. Each one was bone-tired and weighed down with a heavy overcoat, rifle, pistol, and 244 rounds of ammunition.

The temperature was near zero and the wind was howling. It was so cold, said Private Creek, that the spit "froze when it left your mouth."

They rode hard all night, making just three brief

halts to give the horses a rest, and reached the agency at 5:30 A.M. They had ridden an incredible eighty-four miles in a little over seven and a half hours.

Several of the soldiers were about two miles behind the main group, riding guard on the supply wagons. Suddenly they were attacked by a large force of warriors, and in the first exchange of shots, Private Charles Haywood was killed.

Captain John Loud asked two Indian scouts to "carry a message for assistance" to the agency, but they "declined to do so."

Corporal William Wilson "volunteered to take the message and did so successfully, although Indians could be seen plainly endeavoring to cut him off from reaching the Agency."

When Wilson told the soldiers of the attack, they quickly saddled up and rode out to the rescue of their comrades.

No sooner had they returned to camp, however, than a courier came riding in shouting that the 7th was in danger of being annihilated. The black troopers mounted up again and urged their horses toward the sound of gunfire and the sight of swirling smoke.

When they reached the valley where the 7th was pinned down by warriors, they split into two columns: Corporal Wilson and half the soldiers charged their horses up the east side of the valley, while Sergeant George Jordan and the others dismounted and ran up the west side.

The warriors fell back while the Buffalo Soldiers pursued them, and members of the 7th scrambled to safety "under cover of the Hotchkiss guns."

For all practical purposes the fighting on the Pine Ridge Reservation was over, and the Native American struggle to hold on to the land was also over.

There were still thousands of men, women and children hiding in the Badlands, but soon they would come in. Almost in the blinking of an eye, everything had changed for the Lakotas.

Three decades before, millions of buffalo roamed the Plains as thick as the stars in the Road of Ghosts (the Milky Way), and most of the people were as free as the animals that gave them food, clothing, and shelter.

Now the buffalo were gone, and men who once hunted them were struggling to keep their families from starving.

Forty-five men, who had returned from Buffalo Bill's "Wild West" show just a few weeks before the massacre, helped the army hunt down the Ghost Dancers in return for $13 a month plus rations.

On January 21, General Miles held a grand review at Pine Ridge. All the regiments marched past, joined by Lakota and Cheyenne army scouts. When the Buffalo Soldiers appeared, Miles raised his white-gloved hand in salute.

The men of the 9th, who had been the first to arrive at Pine Ridge, were the last to leave.

Sometimes the Buffalo Soldiers rode past a church where they had taken wounded Lakota men, women, and children after the massacre.

The black cavalrymen "treated them well," said Private Simpson Mann of Company F, but seven of the wounded bled to death on the straw-covered floor.

The last sights the dying people saw were Christmas wreaths hanging from the rafters and a crudely lettered banner hanging above the pulpit that read: PEACE ON EARTH, GOOD WILL TO MEN.

Seventeen white soldiers, including the officers in charge of the Hotchkiss guns at Wounded Knee Creek, were given Congressional Medals of Honor. Corporal Wilson was also awarded the medal.

The Buffalo Soldiers stayed on the reservation until March and were then sent back to their forts in Kansas, Wyoming, and Utah.

Sergeant Jordan and his comrades were briefly transferred to Fort Myers, Virginia, as a "reward" for their service. It marked the first time a unit of the Buffalo Soldiers had been allowed east of the Mississippi River.

The troopers served as honorary guards over the nation's capital for several months. But most white Americans still objected to the presence of armed black men near large cities, so authorities transferred the men back to Fort Robinson.

The men of the 10th continued to occupy the most desolate posts in the Southwest.

The lodges and the campfires and the cavalrymen's long marches were mostly memories after Pine Ridge.

Gone also were the hopes held by so many men and women less than thirty years before: the hopes of Native Americans that they could somehow hold on to the freedom they had always known, and the hopes of the Buffalo Soldiers that their courage would earn them and their loved ones a freedom they had never known.

More than anyone could have imagined, the raw young recruits who rode into the Great Plains that first summer and fall of 1867, "dreaming of the red man and the bison," had truly ridden into the Time of the Changing Seasons.

It was the time of Crazy Horse and Geronimo, of Custer and Mackenzie, and of buffalo herds that numbered in the millions and shook the earth with the thunder of their charges.

It was a time when legends of cavalrymen and cowboys and warriors were created, and history was changed forever.

But as much as anything else, for almost thirty years in that vast expanse of land that still echoes with their passing, it was the Time of the Buffalo Soldiers.

Epilogue

The Buffalo Soldiers spent more time fighting in the West than any other cavalry regiments in the United States Army, and their courage and sacrifices helped create the United States that we now know.

When they first rode out of the forts in 1867, all of the Great Plains except Texas, Kansas, and Nebraska were still territories. By the time the Buffalo Soldiers were transferred to Cuba in 1898 to fight in the Spanish-American War, they had helped lay the groundwork for the creation of eight more states: Colorado, North Dakota, South Dakota, Montana, Utah, Oklahoma, New Mexico, and Arizona.

Many of the men retired in the West and helped build small black communities near army posts from Nebraska and Montana in the north to Texas and Arizona in the south.

George Jordan retired to Crawford, Nebraska, in 1897 and became the recognized leader of the town's small black community. He and the other soldiers looked after each other to an impressive degree.

When Caleb Benson was partially blinded after a stove blew up in his face at Fort Robinson, the army gave the twenty-seven-year veteran a medical discharge. For almost three years, while Benson tried unsuccessfully to find work, the men of his former company supported him.

Several of the men used their skill with horses to hire on as broncobusters at ranches throughout the Great Plains or, like some of the warriors they once battled, tried to build new lives as farmers on land that had seen so much death and destruction.

The summer following the massacre at Wounded Knee, the place where so many people had died was turned into a farm by a Lakota warrior named Bull Eagle.

"My friends," he told visiting U.S. commissioners, "this piece of land on the other side of the creek which has been flooded with blood is where I make my home. . . . I am still walking through the field and plowing up the ground, covering up the blood."

Not far to the south, in Sioux County, Nebraska, some of the retired Buffalo Soldiers also turned to farming.

Henry McClain was one of them.

He and his wife, Louisa, managed to support two adopted children, as well as five of McClain's brothers and sisters, on their small farm not far from Fort Robinson.

When the old cavalryman died in 1907, the local newspaper praised him for "his manhood and integrity."

The same praise could have been given to many of the men McClain served with, but the Buffalo Soldiers were rarely praised.

No deed they performed was strong enough to change the hatred they encountered or to make a dent in the walls of racism. Among the first steps taken in every state the soldiers helped create were the passage of laws calling for rigid racial segregation in virtually every aspect of life.

Like the black soldiers in the Civil War, the Buffalo Soldiers had dreamed of creating a country that respected them and their people.

"He who fights the battles of America, may claim America as his country and have that claim respected," Frederick Douglass told black men in urging them to join the Union Army during the Civil War.

But that claim had not been respected for the black soldiers who fought in the Civil War, and it was not respected for the Buffalo Soldiers who fought on the Great Plains.

In 1898, the 9th and 10th fought in the Spanish-American War in Cuba. They helped save Theodore Roosevelt's Rough Riders, and won five Congressional Medals of Honor for their valor.

But a few months later, Roosevelt told white audiences the Buffalo Soldiers were cowards who were "peculiarly dependent on their white officers" and that black people "were altogether inferior to the whites."

A historian once said of the Buffalo Soldiers: "Why they went on, why they went through the agonies of hell for a nation that kicked them at every turn, is almost beyond human analysis."

"We Negroes had little, at the turn of the century, to help sustain our faith in ourselves except the pride that we took in the Ninth and Tenth Cavalry, the Twenty-fourth and Twenty-fifth Infantry," historian Rayford W. Logan wrote years later.

"Many Negro homes had prints of the famous charge of the colored troops up San Juan Hill. They were our Ralph Bunche, Marian Anderson, Joe Louis, and Jackie Robinson."

In his farewell address to the men of the 10th in 1888, after commanding them for twenty-two years, Colonel Grierson predicted that the Buffalo Soldiers' service to their country "cannot fail — sooner or later — to meet with due recognition and reward."

This seemed unlikely to men who were never even given a regimental flag by the army they served and had to make their own.

But on July 28, 1992, on the 126th anniversary of the day Congress authorized creation of the

Buffalo Soldier regiments, the Buffalo Soldier Monument was unveiled at Fort Leavenworth.

There on the post where Grierson was once ordered to take his "damned Mokes and camp outside," there now stands an almost thirteen-foot-tall statue of a black cavalryman astride a horse.

On a walkway surrounding the statue are markers honoring the eighteen black soldiers who won the Congressional Medal of Honor on the Great Plains of the American West.

"This is symbolic of all the unsung heroes out of time," said sculptor Eddie Dixon of the statue he created.

General Colin A. Powell, the black chairman of the Joint Chiefs of Staff and the highest-ranking black officer in the history of the United States, dedicated the monument.

"Look at him," Powell declared. "Soldier of the nation. Eagles on his buttons, crossed sabres on his canteen, a rifle in his hand, a pistol on his hip. Courageous, iron will.

"He was every bit the soldier that his white brother was. He showed that the theory of inequality must be wrong. He could not be denied his right. It might take time; it did take time. But he knew that in the end he could not be denied."

Today, in the shadow of the mountains where the soldiers battled Victorio in 1880, the stone "forts" the soldiers built stand almost exactly as they did on that long-ago day.

The earth still remembers the Buffalo Soldiers, even if most men do not.

Fittingly enough for men who rode tens of thousands of miles on horseback, the Buffalo Soldiers were the last men on horseback in the U.S. Army.

In the first years of World War II, they urged their mounts along rugged trails on the southwestern border with Mexico, just as their predecessors had ridden the same trails decades before. Instead of searching for Geronimo, Nana, or Victorio, however, the last of the Buffalo Soldiers were on guard against a possible Japanese invasion.

The Buffalo Soldier, said Powell, "believed that hatred and bigotry and prejudice could not defeat him, that through his pain and sacrifice they would be destroyed for the evil things they are," and that "someday through his efforts and the efforts of others to follow, future generations would know full freedom."

It is far too late for the troopers Grierson commanded to share in the "due recognition and reward" that have finally come their way.

But there is still time for others to learn the story of those brave young men who left the forts so long ago, on their long ride into history.

Black Congressional Medal of Honor Winners in the West

1. Sgt. Emanuel Stance (Ninth Cavalry), May 20–21, 1870. Near Kickapoo Springs, Texas.

2. Pvt. Adam Paine (Seminole-Negro Indian Scouts), Sept. 20, 1874. The Staked Plains, Texas.

3. Pvt. Pompey Factor (Seminole-Negro Indian Scouts), April 25, 1875. Near Eagle's Nest Crossing on the Pecos River, Texas.

4. Pvt. Isaac Payne (Seminole-Negro Indian Scouts), April 25, 1875. Near Eagle's Nest Crossing on the Pecos River, Texas.

5. Sgt. John Ward (Seminole-Negro Indian Scouts), April 25, 1875. Near Eagle's Nest Crossing on the Pecos River, Texas.

6. Cpl. Clinton Greaves (Ninth Cavalry), Jan. 24, 1877. Florida Mountains, New Mexico.

7. Sgt. Thomas Boyne (Ninth Cavalry), May 29, 1879, Mimbres Mountains, New Mexico, and Sept. 27, 1879, Cuchillo Negro Creek, New Mexico.

8. Sgt. John Denny (Ninth Cavalry), Sept. 18, 1879. Las Animas Canyon, New Mexico.

9. Sgt. Henry Johnson (Ninth Cavalry), Oct. 2–5, 1879. Milk River, Colorado.

10. Sgt. George Jordan (Ninth Cavalry), May 14, 1880, Old Fort Tularosa, New Mexico, and Aug. 12, 1881, Carizzo Canyon, New Mexico.

11. Sgt. Thomas Shaw (Ninth Cavalry), Aug. 12, 1881. Carizzo Canyon, New Mexico.

12. 1st Sgt. Moses Williams (Ninth Cavalry), Aug. 16, 1881. Cuchillo Negro Mountains, New Mexico.

13. Pvt. Augustus Walley (Ninth Cavalry), Aug. 16, 1881. Cuchillo Negro Mountains, New Mexico.

14. Sgt. Brent Woods (Ninth Cavalry), Aug. 19, 1881. Cuchillo Negro Mountains, New Mexico.

15. Sgt. Benjamin Brown (Twenty-fourth Infantry), May 11, 1889. Between Fort Grant and Fort Thomas, Arizona.

16. Cpl. Isaiah Mays (Twenty-fourth Infantry), May 11, 1889. Between Fort Grant and Fort Thomas, Arizona.

17. Sgt. William McBryar (Tenth Cavalry), March 7, 1890. Salt River, Arizona.

18. Cpl. William O. Wilson (Ninth Cavalry), Dec. 30, 1890. Pine Ridge Reservation, South Dakota.

(Two white officers also won Medals of Honor: 2nd Lt. Powhattan H. Clarke [10th], May 3, 1886, Pinito Mountains, Mexico; and 2nd Lt. George R. Burnett [9th], Aug. 16, 1881, Cuchillo Negro Mountains, New Mexico.)

Bibliography

1. Barrett, S. M., ed. *Geronimo: His Own Story*. New York: E. P. Dutton & Co., Inc., 1970.
2. Billington, Monroe Lee. *New Mexico's Buffalo Soldiers, 1866–1900*. Niwot: University of Colorado Press, 1991.
3. Bogue, Phillips, Wright, eds., *The West of the American People*. (Contains article, "The Black Regulars," by Thomas D. Phillips.) Itasca: F. E. Peacock Publishers, 1970.
4. Brown, Dee. *Bury My Heart at Wounded Knee*. New York: Henry Holt and Company, 1970.
5. Cantor, George. *Historic Landmarks of Black America*. Detroit: Gale Research Inc., 1991.
6. Carroll, John M., ed. *The Black Military Experience in the American West*. New York: Liveright Publishing Corp., 1971.
7. Debo, Angie. *Geronimo: The Man, His Time, His Place*. Norman: University of Oklahoma Press, 1976.
8. Downey, Fairfax. *The Buffalo Soldiers in the Indian Wars*. New York: McGraw-Hill Book Company, 1969.
9. Drotning, Phillip T. *Black Heroes in Our Nation's History*. New York: Cowles Book Co., Inc., 1969.
10. Flipper, Henry O. *Negro Frontiersman*. El Paso: Texas Western College Press, 1963.
11. Foner, Jack D. *Blacks and the Military in American His-*

tory. New York: Praeger Publishers, 1974.

12. Franklin, John Hope. *George Washington Williams: A Biography.* Chicago: The University of Chicago Press, 1985.

13. Freedman, Russell. *Indian Chiefs.* New York: Holiday House, 1987.

14. Jensen, Richard E., Paul, R. Eli, and Carter, John E. *Eyewitness at Wounded Knee.* Lincoln: University of Nebraska Press, 1991.

15. Katz, William Loren. *Black Indians: A Hidden Heritage.* New York: Atheneum, 1986.

16. ———. *Black People Who Made the Old West.* New York: Thomas Y. Crowell Co., 1977.

17. Leckie, William H. *The Buffalo Soldiers: A Narrative of the Negro Cavalry in the West.* Norman: University of Oklahoma Press, 1967.

18. Lindenmeyer, Otto. *Black & Brave: The Black Soldier in America.* New York: McGraw-Hill Book Company, 1970.

19. Logan, Rayford W. *The Betrayal of the Negro.* New York: Macmillan, 1970.

20. ——— and Winston, Michael R., eds. *Dictionary of American Negro Biography.* New York: W. W. Norton & Company, 1982.

21. Monaghan, Jay. *Custer: The Life of General George Armstrong Custer.* Boston: Little, Brown and Company, 1959.

22. Painter, Neil Irvin. *Exodusters: Black Migration to Kansas after Reconstruction.* New York: W.W. Norton & Company, Inc., 1992.

23. Rice, Lawrence D. *The Negro in Texas, 1874–1900.* Baton Rouge: Lousiana State University Press, 1971.

24. Sandoz, Mari. *Crazy Horse: The Strange Man of the Oglalas.* Lincoln: University of Nebraska Press, 1961.

25. Williams, George W. *History of the Negro Race in America from 1619 to 1880: Negroes as Slaves, as Soldiers, and as Citizens*, 2 vols. in one. New York: Arno Press and *The New York Times*, 1968.

PERIODICALS:

1. Brininstool, E. A. "The Beecher Island Fight" (as related to Brininstool by scout John Hurst), *Winners of the West*, July 1940, pp. 1, 4, 7, 8.
   (*Winners of the West* was a bulletin published in St. Louis, Missouri, from 1923 to 1940 "in the Interest of the Survivors of Indian Wars and the Old Army of the Plains." The largest collection of *Winners* is in The Bancroft Library, University of California, Berkeley.)
2. Carpenter, Col. L. H. "The Story of a Rescue," *Winners of the West*," February 28, 1934, p. 4.
   (There are items by and about George W. Ford, the last surviving member of the original Buffalo Soldiers, in the September 1928, June 1938, and August 1939 issues of *Winners of the West*. There are letters and articles by Reuben Waller in the February 1934, May 1929, March 1930, and November 1933 issues.)
3. *Harper's Weekly*. "Our Indian Sketches," Vol. XI, No. 558 (September 7, 1867), p. 564.
4. Hunter, John W. "A Trooper of the Ninth Cavalry," *Frontier Times*, IV (April 1927), pp. 9–11.
5. Lowe, Albert S. "Camp Life of the Tenth U.S. Cavalry," *The Colored American Magazine*, Vol. 7, No. 3 (1904), pp. 203–208.
6. McConnell, Roland C. "Isaiah Dorman and the Custer Expedition," *Journal of Negro History*, XXXIII (July 1948), pp. 344–352.
7. Nunn, W. Curtis. "Eighty-six Hours Without Water on

the Texas Plains," *Southwestern Historical Quarterly*, XLIII (January 1940), pp. 356–364.

8. Perry, Alex W. "The Ninth United States Cavalry in the Sioux Campaign of 1890," *Journal of the U.S. Cavalry Association*, IV (1891), pp. 37–40.

9. Porter, Kenneth Wiggins. "The Seminole Negro-Indian Scouts, 1870–1881," *Southwestern Historical Quarterly*, LV (January 1952), pp. 358–377.

10. ————. "Negroes and Indians on the Texas Frontier," *Southwestern Historical Quarterly*, Vol. LIII (October 1949).

11. Rickey, Don, Jr. Interview of Private Simpson Mann of the 9th Cavalry, February, 1965. Provided courtesy of the Fort Robinson Museum, Crawford, Nebraska.

12. Savage, Sherman W. "The Role of Negro Soldiers in Protecting the Indian Frontier from Intruders," *Journal of Negro History*, Vol. XXXVI (January 1951), pp. 25–34.

13. Schubert, Frank N. "The Violent World of Emanuel Stance, Fort Robinson, 1887," *Nebraska History*, Vol. LV (Summer 1974), pp. 203–219.

14. ————. "Black Soldiers on the White Frontier: Some Factors Influencing Race Relations," *Phylon*, Vol. XXXII (Winter 1971), pp. 410–416.

15. ————. "Fort Robinson, Nebraska: The History of a Military Community, 1874–1916." Doctoral dissertation submitted to the Department of History and the Graduate School of the University of Toledo, 1976. Provided courtesy of the Fort Robinson Museum, Crawford, Nebraska.

16. Thompson, Erwin N. "The Negro Soldiers on the Frontier: A Fort Davis Case Study." *Journal of the West*, VII (April 1968), pp. 217–235.

17. Author Unknown. "List of Actions, etc., with Indians and Other Marauders, Participated in by the Tenth U.S.

Cavalry, Chronologically Arranged — 1867–1897,"
Journal of the U.S. Cavalry Association (December 1897),
pp. 499–521.

NEWSPAPERS:

1. Cincinnati *Commercial*. "Military Life on the Plains,"
   by George Washington Williams under the pseudonym,
   Aristides. January 6, 1877. (Cincinnati *Commercial* articles courtesy of the Public Library of Cincinnati &
   Hamilton County, Cincinnati, Ohio.)
2. Cincinnati *Commercial*. "A Winter on the Rio Grande,"
   by George Washington Williams under the pseudonym,
   Aristides. January 13, 1877.
3. *Colored Citizen* (Fort Scott, Kansas), 1878–1879. Brief
   items about black soldiers and civilians throughout the
   Great Plains. Also in-depth articles describing the home-
   steading and other activities of recent black immigrants
   to Kansas.

GOVERNMENT PUBLICATIONS:

1. *Military Service Records: A Select Catalog of National Archives Microfilm Publications*. National Archives Trust
   Fund Board, Washington, D.C., 1985.
   The following are all microfilm publications available
   from the National Archives, Washington, D.C.:
2. *The Negro in the Military Service of the United States,
   1639–1886*. M858.
3. *Historical Sketch, Tenth United States Cavalry, 1866–
   1892, And Report of Operations, Spanish-American War,
   1898*, compiled from official records by Major John
   Bigelow, Jr. Roll 933 from National Archives Publication
   NM-93.

4. *Returns from Regular Army Cavalry Regiments, 1833–1916.* M744. (9th Cavalry Returns from 1866–1895 are on Rolls 87–90. 10th Cavalry Returns from 1866–1896 are on Rolls 95–98.)
5. *Documents Relating to the Military and Naval Service of Blacks Awarded the Congressional Medal of Honor from the Civil War to the Spanish-American War.* M929.
6. *Registers of Enlistments in the United States Army, 1798–1914.* M233.
7. *Returns from United States Military Posts, 1800–1916.* M617.

Picture Credits

Index

Adobe Walls (trading post), attack on, 72–73

African Americans. *See also* Prejudice: allowed in Army (U.S.), 2–5; cowboys and, 85, 160; Custer, George Armstrong and, 25; frontier and, vii–viii; Native Americans and, 8–9, 28–29, 44–45; oppression of, ix–x; western settlement by, 140, 141

Alchise (Apache warrior), 128–129

Apache, Fort, 127

Apache Nation, ix, 19, 21, 32, 86, 137; attacks and raids by, 58, 72, 85, 90, 97–98, 121, 130; Buffalo Soldiers and, 50, 51, 53, 95, 96, 108–110; chiefs of, arrested, 98–99; Geronimo flees reservation, 111; imprisonment of, 129, 132–133; populations of, 136; pursuit of, 127–128, 130–132; removal of, 133–135; reservation system and, 96–97, 98–99, 100, 126; surrender of, 129, 132, 135, 137; Victorio's War and, 100–108; white settlers and, 96–97

Arapaho Nation, 1, 11, 19, 40–41, 43, 138; attacks and raids by, 30, 66; Buffalo Soldiers protect, 46; Indian Peace Commission and, 21, 22; reservation system and, 27; surrender of, 48

Arbuckle, Fort, 24, 26

Army (U.S.). *See also* Buffalo Soldiers; Ninth Cavalry Regiment; Seventh Cavalry Regiment; Tenth Cavalry Regiment: African Americans in, ix, 2–3, 5–6; casualties, 39; cavalry units of, 17; desertions and, 24–25, 45; duties of, 1–2; payroll robbery, 144–146; recruits in, 1

Bayard, Fort, 97, 98

Belknap, Fort, 58

Betters, James, 99–100

Big Bow (Native American chief), 60

Big Foot (Lakota chief), 149; arrest of, 151–152; death of, 152; pursuit of, 150

Big Tree (Native American chief): arrest of, 60, 61; attacks by, 58, 59; imprisonment of, 65, 66; surrender of, 79; trial of, 64–65

Bivins, Horace W., Jr., 140–141

Black Coyote (Cheyenne warrior), 152

Black Horse (Comanche chief), 79, 90

Black Kettle (Cheyenne chief), 30–31, 33, 39–40; death of, 42–43, 44, 45; peace talks by, 40–41

Bonito (Apache warrior), 102

Bowie, Fort, 132

Buell, George, 76–78

Buffalo: commercial uses of, 68–69;

Buffalo (*cont.*)
  Native Americans and, 16; slaughter
    of, x, 27, 29, 53–54, 67, 69–70,
    83, 155
Buffalo Soldiers. *See also* Army (U.S.);
    Ninth Cavalry Regiment; Seventh
    Cavalry Regiment; Tenth Cavalry
    Regiment: Apache Nation and,
    133–135; casualties among, 13–14,
    15, 34, 131; courage of, 55, 159; de-
    sertions among, 24–25, 44; duties
    of, 48, 50, 52, 121–122; frontier
    and, viii–x; Geronimo pursued by,
    127–128; inexperience of, 9–10;
    Lakota Nation and, 153–155; mar-
    riages of, 114; monument honoring,
    162–163; origin of name, 15–16;
    pay of, 4; Pine Ridge Reservation
    and, 140, 148, 150, 156; race preju-
    dice and, 112, 113–120, 156–157,
    161, 162. *See also* Prejudice; recruits
    for, 5–9; Red River War and, 72–
    84; retirement of, 159–161; Spanish-
    American War and, 159, 161–162;
    Staked Plains and, 86–90; training
    of, 10; Victorio's War and, 100–
    108; World War II and, 164
Bull Bear (Native American chief), 43
Bull Eagle (Lakota warrior), 160

Carpenter, Louis, 35, 36, 38, 49
Catch-the-Bear (Ghost Dancer), 149
Chato (Apache warrior), 126, 128–
    129, 132–133
Cherokee Bil (Goldsby, Crawford),
    114
Cherokee Nation, 8, 28
Cheyenne Nation, ix, 11, 19, 36, 40–
    41, 137; attacks and raids by, 12–
    13, 30, 34, 35, 37, 66, 72; Buffalo
    Soldiers protect, 46; campaigns
    against, 33, 39–40, 41–43, 44; cas-
    ualties among, 38, 39, 42; Indian
    Peace Commission and, 21, 22; Red
    River War and, 74, 76, 78, 79–81;
    reservation system and, 27; surrender
    of, 48
Chickasaw Nation, resettlement of, 28
Chihuahua (Apache chief), 129
Christy, William, 13–14

Civil War (U.S.), ix; African Ameri-
    cans massacred in, 6; African Amer-
    ican soldiers in, 3–4, 5–6, 120,
    161; Five Nations and, 28–29; fron-
    tier and, vii; Texas and, 50
Cobb, Fort, 40, 41, 46
Cochise (Apache chief), vii, 95, 128
Cody, Buffalo Bill, 44, 149, 155
Comanche Nation, 1, 11, 19, 32, 40,
    45, 86, 137; attacks and raids by,
    30, 57, 58, 66, 72, 85, 90; Buffalo
    Soldiers and, 50; campaign against,
    46; Camp Wichita and, 48; hunting
    grounds of, destroyed, 67; Indian
    Peace Commission and, 21, 22; pop-
    ulations of, 136; Red River War
    and, 69–70, 74, 76, 78, 83; reserva-
    tion system and, 27, 53, 54
Concho, Fort, 67, 74, 75, 87, 89, 91,
    112, 114, 116, 123
Congressional Medal of Honor: African
    Americans winning, listed, 165–167;
    Brown, Benjamin awarded, 146; Buf-
    falo Soldiers win in Spanish-
    American War, 161–162; Clarke,
    Powhattan awarded, 131; Denny,
    John awarded, 104; Greaves, Clin-
    ton awarded, 98; Mays, Isaiah
    awarded, 146; Shaw, Thomas
    awarded, 109; Stance, Emanuel
    awarded, 54–55; Wilson, William
    awarded, 156; Woods, Brent
    awarded, 110
Congress (U.S.): African Americans
    allowed in Army by, 2–5; betrayal
    of Native American rights by, 143;
    Indian Peace Commission created
    by, 20; race prejudice and, 118–119,
    120; reservation system and, 27; vot-
    ing rights and, 25
Cooper, Charles, 91, 93, 94
Cowboys, African Americans and, 85,
    160
Crazy Horse (Lakota chief), vii, 11,
    157; imprisonment and death of,
    138; reservation system and, 137–
    138
Creek Nation, resettlement of, 28
Crime. *See also* Violence: Apache Na-
    tion victimized by, 100; army payroll

robbery, 144–146; Buffalo Soldiers and, 50, 53, 68; embezzlement charge against Lt. Flipper, 123–124; stagecoach robberies, 85–86, 142; white settlers and, 49

Crook, George, 126, 127, 129

Crow Nation, vii–viii, 1, 138

Custer, George Armstrong, 12, 24, 157; arrests Native chiefs, 46; Cheyenne campaign of, 41, 43, 44; defeat of, 138, 139; prejudice of, 25

Davis, Fort, 120–121, 125, 126

Denver Post Road, protection of, 34, 35

Desertions: Army and, 24–25, 45; Buffalo Soldiers, 24–25, 44; racial violence and, 114

Dog Soldier Society (Hotamitanio), 34

Eagle Heart (Native American chief), 60

Embezzlement charge, against Lt. Flipper, 123–124

Fast Bear (Native American chief), 60

Five Nations: Buffalo Soldiers assigned to protect, 28–29; resettlement of, 27–28

Flipper, Henry Ossian, 106–107, 122–125

Ford, George W., 7, 26, 40

Forsyth, George, 35–36, 37, 38

Frontier: African Americans and, vii–viii; Buffalo Soldiers and, viii–ix; Civil War (U.S.) and, vii; military protection of, 2–3; violence and, 10, 12–15, 26, 27, 29

Geronimo (Apache chief), vii, viii, 2, 95, 96, 125, 157; arrest of, 98–99; flees reservation, 111, 126–127; imprisonment of, 132; pursuit of, 127–128, 130–132; returns to reservation, 126; surrender of, 129, 132, 135, 137

Ghost Dance: Lakota Nation embraces, 146–149; massacre of followers of, 154–155

Gibson, Fort, 23, 26

Goldsby, Crawford (Cherokee Bill), 114

Goldsby, George, 7, 114

Good Thunder (Lakota chief), 146

Grant, Fort, 127

Grant, Ulysses S., 2, 4, 5, 22, 145–146

Gray Beard (Cheyenne chief), 79

Grierson, Benjamin, 17, 24, 25, 46–47, 49–50, 60, 62, 63, 65, 81, 87, 90, 106, 107, 112, 114, 116, 117, 118, 123, 127, 162, 163, 164

Griffin, Fort, 57, 67, 78

Hams, Thornton, 144–145, 146

Hancock, Winfield Scott, 12, 14, 19, 31

Hatch, Edward, 68, 96, 103

Hays, Fort (Kansas), 12, 14

Hazen, William B., 40–41

Hickok, Wild Bill, 43–44

Hooker, Theodore, 101, 102

Hotamitanio (Dog Soldier Society), 34

Howard, Barney, 90, 93

Hunters (white): buffalo killed by, 27, 68–69; supply lines for, 57; targeted by warriors, 72

Indian Peace Commission, 33; betrayal of terms of, 27, 28, 29–30, 31, 40; Congress creates, 20; Native Americans and, 19, 20–23

Isaai (Kwahadi Comanche prophet), 70

Johnson, Andrew, 25, 31

Jones, Eldridge, 52–53

Jordan, George, 6, 32, 104–105, 109, 118, 140, 154, 156, 159–160

Juh (Apache chief), 96

Kaitsenko people, 63–64

Kansas Pacific Railroad, construction of, 12

Kayitah (Apache scout), 132

Kickapoo Nation, 32, 53

Kicking Bird (Native American chief), 30, 61, 63, 79

Kiowa Nation, 1, 11, 19, 32, 40, 45, 137; arrest of chiefs of, 62; Buffalo

Kiowa Nation (*cont.*)
Soldiers and, 50; Camp Wichita and, 48; hunting grounds of, destroyed, 67; Indian Peace Commission and, 21, 22; populations of, 136; raids and attacks by, 30, 57, 58, 66, 72, 85; Red River War and, 74, 76, 78, 79; reservation system and, 27, 53, 54; surrender of, 46, 47
Kwahadi Comanche Nation: reservation system and, 83; war plans of, 69–70

Lakota (Sioux) Nation, ix, 1, 11, 33; arrest of, 151–152; attacks by, 35, 37; casualties among, 38, 39; Ghost Dance embraced by, 146–149; massacre of, 152–153, 155–156; reservation system and, 137–138, 141–142, 149
Larned, Fort (Kansas), 22
Leavenworth, Fort (Kansas), viii, 17, 163
Lipan Nation, 53, 85
Little Raven (Arapaho chief), 21
Lone Wolf (Kiowa chief), 59; arrest of, 46, 61–62; imprisonment of, 79; Indian Peace Commission and, 21, 22; peace mission of, 66–67; release of, 53; war plans of, 70

Mace, William, 113, 114–115
Mackenzie, Ranald, 63, 64, 86, 157
Mail lines: murder of carriers, 26–27; protection of, 51, 53
Mamanti the Sky Walker (medicine man), 58, 59, 79
Mangas (Apache chief), viii, 2, 130, 135, 136
Marriage: of Buffalo Soldiers, 114
Martine (Apache scout), 132
Massacres: of African Americans, 45, 139; of Lakota Nation (by Army), 152–153; by Native Americans in Kansas, 31; Sand Creek, Colorado (by Army), 21, 40
McCarthy, Tom, 115, 116, 117
McClain, Henry, 160–161
McKavett, Fort, 89
Medicine Lodge Treaty, 82–83; be-

trayal of terms of, 27, 28, 29–30, 31, 40, 49, 60, 69; hunting prohibitions of, 69
Medicine Water (Cheyenne chief), 79
Mescalero Apache Nation, 32; attacks by, 90; Buffalo Soldiers and, 51, 53
Mexican Revolution: Buffalo Soldiers and, 50; raids in Texas and, 85
Mexico, 32; Apache Nation and, 110; Buffalo Soldiers and, 53; Geronimo flees to, 127–128, 130; race prejudice and, 125; slavery and, 108, 132; Victorio's War and, 107–108
Miles Nelson A., 130, 132, 137, 138, 148, 150, 155
Minimic (Cheyenne chief), 79
Morrow, Albert P., 51–52, 55

Nachez (Apache chief), 129
Naiche (Native American chief), 2
Nana (Apache warrior), 108–110, 125–126
Native Americans. *See also entries under specific nations:* African Americans and, 8–9, 28–29, 44–45; frontier and, vii; Indian Peace Commission and, 19, 20–23; land taken from, ix, 11; prejudice against, 127; Sherman, William Tecumseh and, 47; subduing of, 135–136, 137, 155, 157
Ninth Cavalry Regiment, 1. *See also* Army (U.S.); Buffalo Soldiers; Seventh Cavalry Regiment; Tenth Cavalry Regiment; battles of, 54–55; casualties in, 52–53, 101–102, 103; duties of, 32, 50, 52; formation of, 4; New Mexico and, 86, 96, 110; Pine Ridge Reservation and, 148, 156; recruits in, 7, 53; Red River War and, 76; Spanish-American War and, 161–162; Victorio's War and, 101–108
Nolan, Nicholas, 90, 91, 92–95

Ogallala Sioux Nation, 36
Ojo Caliente raid, 101–103
Ord, Edward O., 117–118

Paiute Nation, 146, 147
Palo Duro Canyon, Battle of, 73–75
Pawnee Killer (Lakota chief), 33, 36
Pawnee Nation, 138
Pine Ridge Reservation: Buffalo Soldiers guard, 140, 148, 149; conditions at, 143; Ghost Dance embraced at, 146; white settlers on, 143, 147–148, 149–150
Pope, John, 102, 108
Prejudice. *See also* African Americans: African Americans and, 5, 8–9, 82; Buffalo Soldiers and, 23–24, 47–48, 50–51, 65, 67–68, 101, 102, 112, 118–120, 156–157; Hooker, Theodore and, 101, 102; Native Americans and, 127

Quakers, 60, 65
Quanah Parker (Comanche chief): attacks by, 72; reservation system and, 86, 91; surrender of, 82–83; war plans of, 69, 70
Quitman, Fort, 51–52

Railroads: buffalo slaughter and, 69; cattle trails and, 85; Cheyenne attack on, 12–13; construction of, 12, 29; protection of, 23
Red Cloud (Native American chief), 11, 141, 147, 149
Red River War (1874–75): Adobe Walls attack, 72–73; Battle of Palo Duro Canyon, 73, 74–75; conduct of, 76–78; end of, 78, 82–83; fighting in, 69–71
Reservation system. *See also entries under specific nations*: Apache Nation and, 96–97, 98–99, 100; Indian Peace Commission and, 21, 22–23; land speculation and, 98; life in, 27; Native Americans and, 136; Quanah Parker and, 82–83
Richardson, Fort, 58, 59, 60, 63, 67
Riley, Fort, 10, 17, 23, 25
Robinson, Fort, 137, 140, 141, 142, 143, 157
Roman Nose (Native American chief), viii, 11, 21; attacks by, 33, 35, 36–

37; death of, 37–38, 39; Indian Peace Commission and, 21, 22, 23
Rosebud Reservation, Ghost Dance embraced at, 146

San Angelo, Texas, 112–113, 117
San Antonio-El Paso Road, 51, 53, 90
Sand Creek, Colorado, massacre at, 21, 40
Satank (Native American chief): arrest of, 60–63; attacks by, 58, 59; death of, 63–64
Satanta (Native American chief), viii, 11, 20, 43; arrest of, 46, 60–63; attacks by, 14–15, 58, 59; buffalo hunting and, 54; description of, 14; imprisonment of, 65, 66, 79; Indian Peace Commission and, 21; release of, 53, 67; surrender of, 79; trial of, 64–65; war plans of, 70
Segregation: of African Americans, ix–x; schools and, 119
Seminole Nation, resettlement of, 28
Seminole-Negro scouts, 74, 88
Seventh Cavalry Regiment, 49. *See also* Army (U.S.); Buffalo Soldiers; Ninth Cavalry Regiment; Tenth Cavalry Regiment; Big Foot and, 151; Buffalo Soldiers rescue, 154–155; desertions from, 25; horses and, 24; Lakota massacred by, 151, 152–153; Pine Ridge Reservation and, 150
Shafter, William, 87, 90, 117–118, 123
Sheridan, Philip, 31, 33, 35, 40, 41, 53, 88; Apache and, 96, 129; buffalo hunting and, 69; Cheyenne campaign of, 40, 41, 43
Sherman, William Tecumseh, 58; arrest of chiefs by, 61; attitude toward Indians of, 47, 65, 67, 133; Cheyenne and, 43, 46; Indian Peace Commission and, 20, 22; race prejudice and, 119; Red River War and, 74; reservation system and, 30
Short Bull (Lakota chief), 146
Shoshone Nation, 1, 138
Sill, Fort, 48–49, 53, 59, 65, 67, 75, 78, 79, 82, 86, 90

Sitting Bull (Lakota chief), vii, 11–12, 141–142; murder of, 148–149, 150; Native American culture protected by, 148

Spanish-American War, Buffalo Soldiers and, 159, 161–162

Stagecoach lines: protection of, 51; robberies of, 85–86, 142

Staked Plains: Buffalo Soldiers and, 86; decribed, 87; mapping of, 89–90; water and, 91–94

Stance, Emanuel, 6, 51, 140; awarded Congressional Medal of Honor, 54–55; murder of, 142–143

Stanton, Fort, 100

Stone Calf (Cheyenne chief), 31

Sun Dance ceremony, 69, 147

Supply, Camp, 41, 42, 48, 49, 65, 119

Tall Bull (Cheyenne chief), 36, 37

Tatum, Lawrie, 60, 65

Ten Bears (Comanche chief), 21, 22

Tenth Cavalry Regiment, 1. See also Army (U.S.); Buffalo Soldiers; Ninth Cavalry Regiment; Seventh Cavalry Regiment; casualties in, 13–14, 15, 65; duties of, 23–24, 31–32, 86; Flipper case and, 122–125; formation of, 4; move to Fort Davis, 120–121; prejudice against, 67–68; recruits in, 8; Red River War and, 75–76; roster of, 16–17; Spanish-American War and, 161–162; Staked Plains and, 86–90; Victorio's War and, 106

Texas: race prejudice in, 50–51, 67–68; raids in, 32–33, 55, 57–58, 66

Texas Rangers: racial violence and, 113–114, 115; slavery and, 50; Victorio's War and, 101–102

Thomas, Fort, 127

Tomahawk, Red, 149

Tonkawa scouts, 74, 88

Tosawi (Comanche chief), 47

Trudeau, Pierre, 35, 36

United States Military Academy (West Point), 106, 119, 122

Verde, Fort, 127

Victorio (Apache chief), viii, 2, 135, 163; arrest of, 98–99; attacks by, 98; death of, 108; surrender of, 100; war of, 100–108

Violence. See also Crime: desertions and, 114; frontier and, 10, 12–15, 26, 27, 29; racial; in South, 5, 51, 138–141; Texas, 113–115

Wallace, Fort (Kansas), 34, 35, 36

Waller, Reuben, 6–7, 32, 33, 36, 38–39, 62–63, 70

Water, staked plains and, 87, 89, 91–94

Westward settlement: African Americans and, 140, 141; Apache Nation and, 96–97; military protection and, 2–3, 58, 67; Native American hunting grounds and, 29

Wheeler, James, 144–145, 146

White Horse (Native American chief), 36, 79

Wichita, Camp, 47

Wilks, Jacob, 5, 70, 74–75

Williams, George Washington, 5–6, 9–10, 23, 44–45, 120, 139

Wolf Sleeve (Kiowa-Apache chief), 21

Woman's Heart (Native American chief), 79

World War II, Buffalo Soldiers and, 164

Wounded Knee massacre, 152–153, 155–156, 160

Wovoka (Paiute shaman), 146, 147

Yankton Sioux, 36

ABOUT THE AUTHOR

CLINTON COX is the author of *Undying Glory: The Story of the Massachusetts 54th Regiment*, which was a CBC/NCSS Notable Children's Trade Book in the Field of Social Studies. He has written articles for numerous magazines and newspapers and was twice nominated for the Pulitzer Prize. He received the Page One Award for Best Local Reporting in a Magazine from the Newspaper Guild of New York.

Mr. Cox has both African-American and Native-American ancestry, which made this book particularly interesting yet difficult for him. "The only way I could write this book was to tell it like it happened, trying to show that men do strange things to survive. If not always commendable, I think they can at least always be understandable," he says.

Clinton Cox lives in Schenectady, New York, with his wife.

SCHOLASTIC BIOGRAPHY